An Illustrated History
of the
Knights Templar

D1308001

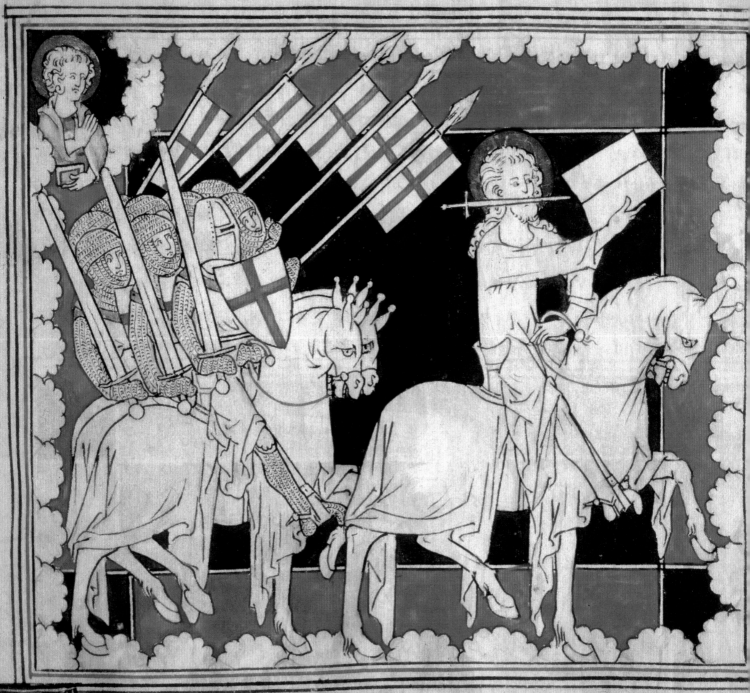

Joo m̄ le ack ouert · 7 cftes vous vn cheoual blanuch · al ge ſiet ſur as anoin
leaux 7 uerreis 7 il uiue en dreiture 7 ſe combat · ces oilz ſiut auſicome

An Illustrated History

of the

Knights Templar

JAMES WASSERMAN

WITH CONTEMPORARY PHOTOS OF
ROME AND JERUSALEM BY STEVEN BROOKE
AND FRANCE BY VERE CHAPPELL

DESTINY BOOKS
Rochester, Vermont

255.9
WAS

Destiny Books
One Park Street
Rochester, Vermont 05767
www.DestinyBooks.com

Destiny Books is a division of Inner Traditions International

Copyright © 2006 by James Wasserman

All rights reserved.
No part of this book may be reproduced or utilized, in any form
or by any means, electronic or mechanical, including photocopying,
recording, or by any information storage and retrieval system,
without permission in writing from the publisher.

Library of Congress Cataloging on Publication Data

Wasserman, James, 1948–
  An illustrated history of the Knights Templar / James Wasserman ; with
contemporary photos of Rome and Jerusalem by Steven Brooke and France by
Vere Chappell.
    p. cm.
  Summary: "A lavishly illustrated, comprehensive look at the mysterious history of
the Order of the Knights Templar"—Provided by publisher.
  Includes bibliographical references and index.
  ISBN-13: 978-1-59477-117-0 (pbk.)
  ISBN-10: 1-59477-117-0 (pbk.)
  1. Templars—History. I. Brooke, Steven. II. Chappell, Vere, 1967– III. Title.
  CR4743.W37 2006
  255'.7913--dc22
                                                    2006016844

Permissions to reproduce the many works of art that appear
in this volume, and their provenance, may be found on pages 185–88.

Book design by Studio 31
www.studio31.com

Frontispiece: Rider on the White Horse (14th century).

Printed and bound in India

10 9 8 7 6 5 4 3 2 1

This book is dedicated to

MY FATHER
Who taught me to respect truth, courage, and integrity—
the values upon which the Templars were founded

JEFF COOPER
Warrior, philosopher, and man of honor,
whose life and writing are an embodiment of those principles

and

RANDY CAIN
Modern master of knighthood's craft

*It seems that a new knightly order
has recently been born in that region,
which is the Orient, once visited
in the flesh from on high.*

*As He then drove out with His
mighty hands the principalities of darkness,
so now does He attack their disciples, the
sons of disobedience, banishing them
by the hands of His protectors.*

Cristo Vino (contemporary painting by Thaedra MabraKhan). This visionary image depicts the central Templar mystery—the fusion of esoteric Christianity with Arabic mysticism, both based on the Wisdom Tradition of Egyptian and Hebrew Qabalah. The artist thus reveals the essence of that mystic Christianity that inspired the hearts, minds, and souls of these brave warriors in their quest for glory and redemption—the true Wine of Christ.

Contents

INTRODUCTION — 10

1 THE FIRST CRUSADE AND VICTORY — 32

2 THE KNIGHTS TEMPLAR ORDER — 37

3 THE GROWTH OF THE KNIGHTS TEMPLAR — 56

4 THE SECOND CRUSADE AND THE SYRIAN ASSASSINS — 69

5 THE RISE OF SALADIN — 79

6 THE THIRD CRUSADE AND RICHARD THE LIONHEARTED — 91

7 THE BYZANTINE CRUSADE — 97

8 THE ALBIGENSIAN HERESY — 101

9 THE FIFTH CRUSADE AND SAINT FRANCIS — 115

10 THE SIXTH CRUSADE AND FREDERICK II — 119

11 THE SEVENTH CRUSADE AND BAYBARS — 127

12 THE EIGHTH AND FINAL CRUSADE — 136

13 THE TEMPLARS IN DEFEAT — 141

14 ARREST AND TRIAL — 151

15 THE TREASURE OF THE KNIGHTS TEMPLAR — 170

MAPS — 180

ACKNOWLEDGMENTS — 182

NOTES TO THE TEXT — 183

PHOTO CREDITS — 185

BIBLIOGRAPHY — 189

INDEX — 190

✤

Introduction

The Knights Templar remain shrouded by an aura of mystery and romance in spite of the massive amount of scholarship devoted to the Order since its founding in 1119. The Templars simply resist the reification of words. They seem to demand immediate access to the living realms of imagination. The inner eye casts itself back to the desert stillness of Israel and witnesses that silence shattered by the thunderous cacophony of armored horses racing to battle. The impact of sword and lance striking armor and shield resounds with the battle cries and trumpet blasts of the medieval warrior, as Christian fights Muslim for possession of a strip of land upon which both their religions were founded. And that war rages fresh to this day—its endless clashes splashed on the pages of every newspaper and television set of the modern world. An American president announces a modern "Crusade"[1] while his enemy identifies the cause for which he fights as "Jihad," a Muslim holy war against "Crusaders and Jews."[2]

The richness of the historical truths of the Knights Templar intertwines inexorably with the myths that have come down through the centuries. The Templars were destroyed as heretics some seven hundred years ago. Yet, from Freemasonry to Ordo Templi Orientis, hierarchical Western secret societies claim derivation from that religious order of warrior-monks established to protect Christian pilgrims as they visited the birthplace of their savior and their faith. Throughout the latter half of the twentieth century especially, the Crusades were frequently dismissed as an outcropping of Western aggression against an undeserving populace. Perhaps the renewed contemporary struggle between Western civilization and the Mideast demands a more sober rethinking of its Act 1, the medieval Crusades.

FIG. I.1. The Fall of Acre (19th century). This painting well captures the fury of that clash of cultures known as the Crusades. The fall of Acre in 1291 marked the defeat of the medieval Christian armies after two centuries of warfare.

The Templar Order was for many years an enormously successful and respected part of European culture, enjoying the singular patronage of Saint Bernard of Clairvaux, medieval Christianity's most influential religious leader. The Knights Templar constituted the pope's private army; for this and many other reasons these elite warriors enjoyed the protection and support of most of the popes to whom they were ultimately responsible. Yet within two hundred years of its founding, the Order was ruthlessly crushed —its leaders tortured and burned at the stake; its members accused of magic, heresy, sexual perversion, and treason; its vast wealth and holdings seized. What happened? And why has their legend persisted so strongly ever since?

A brief look at some of the history preceding the emergence of the Templars after the First Crusade in 1095 will help set the stage to begin to answer these questions, and to reveal ancient causes of today's critical struggle.

Christianity and the Dark Ages

The sixth century marked the beginning of the Dark Ages in western Europe. Life was harsh and brutal. The peasantry, although free, were poor, uneducated, and politically impotent. By the beginning of the seventh century, literacy was reserved for the clergy. Science, medicine, and literature were replaced by magic, superstition, and religious texts. Eighty percent of the population during the Dark Ages never moved more than ten miles from their place of birth. As a result of poor nutrition and medicine, the average life expectancy was thirty years, while the average height for men was not more than five feet three inches. Throughout the ninth and tenth centuries, Europe endured a perpetual state of war, decimated by continuous aggression from

Scandinavian, eastern European, and Germanic tribes, as well as Muslims and Mongols. Savagery and faith, ignorance and piety, agriculture and aggression—this mixture embodied the intellectual stagnation of the Dark Ages.

The rude and unlettered barbarian tribes who had eclipsed the rule of the Roman Empire were led by the Roman Church. The Church provided the glue by which these scattered tribes became a united force capable of protecting the Continent against the military expansion of Islam and the Oriental hordes. Its priests, bishops, and monastic communities provided political as well as spiritual leadership among the far-flung and isolated towns and villages. Ecclesiastical councils served as courts of justice. Christian monasteries preserved learning and literacy. The Church extended the hand of charity to the poor and suffering.

On the other hand, the Church was responsible for inculcating pernicious doctrines that infested Europe for centuries. Original sin was no mere philosophical or religious speculation. The concept of sin informed the entire social, political, and legal structure. Since the human condition was fallen to begin with, justice was, by definition, impossible. Social improvement was not a goal. This was a reversal of earlier Jewish beliefs in the goodness of God and the possibility of reformation of society through adherence to the Divine. To the medieval Christian, life was a test and trial in preparation for death. If one were good, the joys of Paradise followed the loss of the body. The soul-chilling horror of eternal torment in Hell awaited the wicked. Suffering cleansed and purified the soul in preparation for its after-death reward.

Nature herself was evil. She was the source of the insistent, instinctual sexual drive to reproduce. Those conceived by the sin of sex were sin-

FIG. I.2. The Last Judgment (13th century). The medieval mind cowered before the horror of Original Sin, the terror of Hell, and the threat of the Eternal Damnation of the Soul.

ful at birth. Celibacy became a religious demand rather than a spiritual technique. The attempt to promulgate and enforce rigid antisexual behavior on the masses led to a raging rebellion within the European psyche. Insanity and disease are the inevitable consequences of sexual repression, and they took a horrid toll during the Middle Ages. Because sickness of the body was seen as God's punishment for wickedness, the medical arts were confined to Arab and Jewish practitioners and to women, who studied herbs and the healing properties of nature. These were among the many who fell in that great battle against Satan and the flesh known as the Inquisition—the central command center for the centuries of murder, torture, and hysteria that followed its establishment.

While Christianity endured repeated episodes of corruption within its leadership, and while some of its doctrines were clearly responsible for much of the suffering and weakness of Western civilization, it also served a higher purpose. Through the exalted story of Jesus and his holiness, sacrifice, and resurrection, Christianity provided the moral teachings designed to lead many generations of human beings to a higher stage of spiritual evolution.

Feudalism

The savagery of the invasions against Europe during the fifth through tenth centuries encouraged the collectivization of the population under a largely autonomous land-owning nobility. Aristocrats were inclined to leave the targeted cities and establish themselves at their country estates. Independent peasant farmers, or *villeins*, attached themselves to the larger centralized landowners. Ninety percent of the feudal economy was agricultural. Over time, the rich purchased peasant lands and instituted an elaborate system of tenant farming in return for military protection and the physical safety offered by fortified castles. A series of villages grew up around the great estates.

Vassals or retainers were free men of limited means who attached themselves to lords by an act of homage and a vow of fealty, and who provided military service or personal attendance in exchange for protection, land (a fief), and some-

times serfs. The word *vassal* comes from the Celtic word meaning "boy." During the sixth and seventh centuries, vassals were essentially teenage gangs attached to various warlords. They would be sent to do the nefarious bidding of their noble masters, receiving financial support in return. As the concept of the mounted cavalry evolved during the eighth century, the position of the hired warrior was elevated. The enormous expense associated with arming and equipping the mounted knight caused nobles to endow them with lands and peasants by which they could earn their own support.

The king occupied the top of the feudal hierarchy. He was the lord of all vassals. His position was buttressed by several millennia of tradition inherited from the Mediterranean roots of Western civilization regarding the sacred kingship of the realm. Yet the position of feudal kings depended far more on the willing support of their vassals than in either earlier or later centuries. The autonomy of feudal lords functioned as a check on European monarchs for a thousand years. The king was first among relative equals.

Fig. I.3. Jousting practice (14th century). Young men refining their skills with contemporary weapons.

In theory he owned all the land in his realm, while in practice his own landholdings were often no larger than those of his lords.

The tug-of-war between king and nobles is the story of the establishment of the nation-state. As commerce began to develop in Europe during the waning years of the Dark Ages, a wealthy class arose outside the traditional boundaries of the feudal system. This new merchant class demanded centralized stability to rein in the chaos and lawlessness such disparate holding of power encouraged. The merchants achieved their goals by financing the centralized power of the king against the nobles. Popes also found that dealing with individual kings could be less unpredictable than trying to work with groups of barons, so they too promoted the growth of the monarchy. Finally, the fractious nobles were frequently all too unwilling to maintain order and discipline among themselves, as centuries of privilege had inbred arrogance. The tide of history was turning against them, and by the end of the thirteenth century, the French king had triumphed over both nobles and pope to reign supreme over his realm. By 1500, monarchy was the primary form of government in Europe.

CHIVALRY

Chivalry, which developed from a combination of Germanic military codes, Muslim warrior ideals, and Christian devotion, marked the creative high point of feudalism. Beginning in the late eleventh century, its myths were spread and its praises hymned by troubadour minstrel poets who wandered throughout the Languedoc region of southern France. The elite mounted and armored cavalry in service to feudal nobles and devoted to the arts of war were imbued with an inspiring ideology.

While the concept of a military elite remains a contemporary archetype, it was a more formalized and widespread cultural phenomenon during the period of chivalry. For example, the medieval tournaments began as training exercises in the techniques of battle. In time, tournaments evolved into elaborate affairs that could last up to a week, serving as festive communal events of great pageantry and offering opportunities for social and commercial interaction as well as entertainment. Poetry, song, and dance added to the romance of these gala events. Heraldry was a by-product of the tournament. The armored and vizored knights developed graphic symbol sets, unique emblems painted on shields or embroidered on banners, to identify themselves.

The order of knighthood was open to the noble-born candidate, who was received only after completing a long apprenticeship. At the age of seven or eight, the youth began his training as a page. He went on to become a squire between the ages of twelve and fourteen. Vows of Christian fealty overlay the institution of knighthood. The ceremony of induction began with a day of fasting, a ritual bath of purification, a night spent in solitary prayer, confession, and communion. The knight-to-be's sword was blessed by a priest. His liege lord then administered the oath of knighthood and the accolade of reception.

Protection of the weak, courtesy, honor, truthfulness, defense of the Church, chastity, and courage were all elements of the code of chivalry. Romantic love—the idealization of the beloved—was another aspect. The knight pledged himself to a noble lady to whom his efforts were dedicated. While service to the chivalric lady shared many aspects with the devotion accorded to the Virgin Mary, there was a definite sexual element. Medieval marriage was based more on property than love. When troubadours hymned their love for a lady, she was often a married woman. A joyless marriage frequently left open the door to

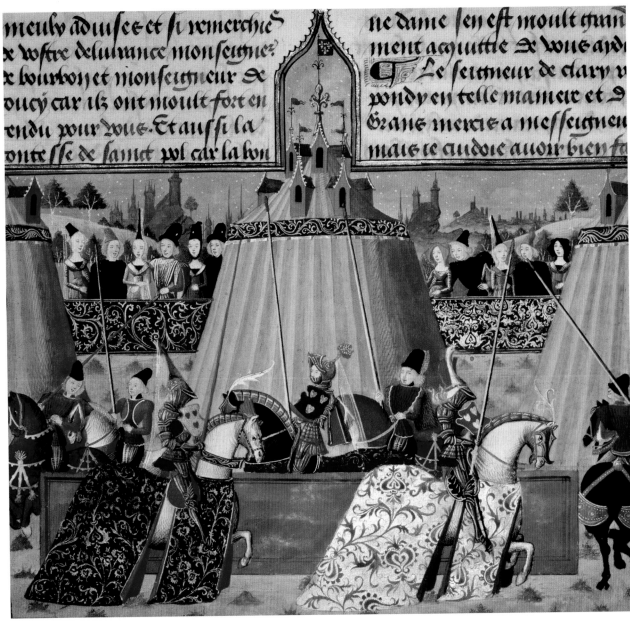

FIG. I.4. Medieval tournament (15th century). These were gala affairs. The classic novel *Ivanhoe* by Sir Walter Scott presents a well-crafted picture of the elaborate and stylized nature of such gatherings, as *Parzival* by Wolfram von Eschenbach does of their martial fury.

an adulterous tryst with her devoted knight or poet.

Chivalrous Grail literature popularized by twelfth-century troubadours introduced themes of the mystic quest interspersed with images of romantic love. Personalized romantic love was heretofore unknown in Western culture. The medieval celebration of emotional and senti-

mental love, accompanied by the chivalric idealization of the feminine, was a marked departure from the utilitarian impersonality with which women had previously been viewed. The elevation of the uniqueness of romantic love focused

FIG. I.5. Kneeling Crusader (12th century). This image conveys the religious dimension of the chivalric ideal.

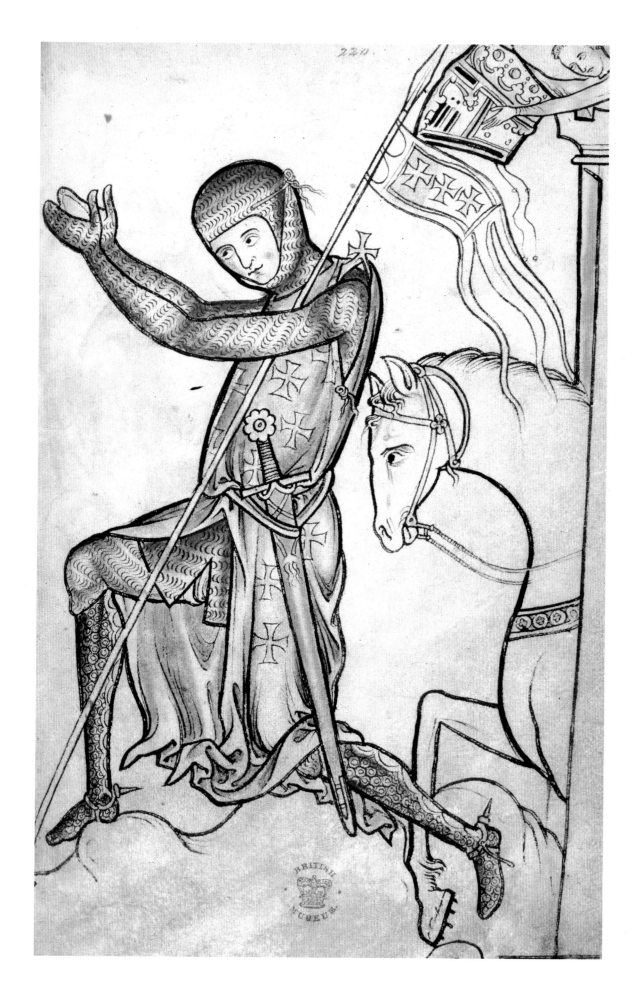

FIG. I.6. Knights in battle at a tournament (14th century). The shield and arms carried by each knight identified him to friend and foe alike.

the medieval mind on the needs and wants of the individual. This represented a complete rebellion against the collective and rigidly stratified feudal social structure.

There was, of course, a darker side to the culture of knighthood. In theory the purpose of the knight was to protect his homeland against foreign invasion. The reality, however, was of interminable infighting among rival feudal lords. Feudal battles were more common but less deadly than modern wars. In addition, the aggressive mounted troops were often guilty of the excesses common to an armed elite set over an unarmed citizenry. The Church attempted to protect the people from the bullying and battling of the knights and nobles by instituting the Peace of God movement as early as the eleventh century.

FIG. I.7. Tournaments and homicide (14th century). The battles fought during tournaments were often fatal. Imagine modern football played with deadly weapons. Here demons inspire and rejoice at the carnage.

Nobles were encouraged to arbitrate their differences and forswear fighting on certain days.

THE RISE OF ISLAM

The Prophet Muhammad was born in Mecca about 570 A.D. His birth and entire life were attended with many signs of divine protection and repeated evidence of angelic intervention and guidance. Numerous miracles were ascribed to him or occurred on his behalf. He was said to be handsome, of medium stature, well mannered, and eloquent, with a perfect command of Arabic and possessed of a natural charismatic radiance. His lineage was of the highest Arab tribal nobility, but the death of his father before his birth, and of his mother when he was six, left him an orphan raised in material simplicity by his paternal grandfather. As he grew to young manhood, Muhammad became a merchant renowned for his integrity.

Soon after he reached the age of thirty-five, Muhammad began to experience what he called "true visions," which caused him periodically to seek the solitude of a cave for meditation. He began his teachings of submission *(islam)* to Allah in about 613. He was visited by the archangel Gabriel, who announced that Muhammad was the messenger of God, and began to receive the verses of the sacred text known as the Koran. Sometime in 620, Muhammad had a nocturnal vision in which he was transported to Jerusalem, where he mounted a winged steed and ascended to Heaven. In the morning he awoke safely in his bed in Mecca. This experience caused Jerusalem to be regarded as the third holy city of Islam, in addition to Mecca and Medina (where Muhammad had begun the second phase of his teaching in 622). Muslim prayers were originally made while facing Jerusalem. In 630, Muhammad's army took Mecca, which he

FIG. I.8. Muhammad (19th century). An idealized portrait of the founder of Islam.

declared to be the Holy City of Islam. He cleansed the Kaaba of idols and proclaimed that no unbeliever should again set foot in the city.[3]

Muhammad extended the new religion through conquest. The martial nature of Islam—with its code of honor and the chivalrous character of its founder—naturally appealed to the warrior culture of the desert tribes of Arabia, who rapidly embraced the new faith. Muhammad stamped out the influence of earlier idolatrous Arab religions, replacing them with his monotheistic Muslim creed. Islam introduced a sense of national and racial unity among the scattered tribes of Arabia for the first time. When Muhammad died in 632, the Muslim faith was firmly established.

The basic unit of political organization among the Arabs was the tribe, to whom intense loyalty and devotion were accorded, and among which were frequent violent conflicts. Arabs were vigorous traders. Nearly 80 percent of the

FIG. I.9. The Kaaba (19th century). During the annual Hajj pilgrimage, Muslims the world over travel to Mecca to gather and ritually circle the most sacred shrine of their faith. The Hajj is the Fifth Pillar of Islam. It is considered a religious obligation to make this pilgrimage at least once during one's lifetime (if one is physically able to do so).

population at the time were Bedouins, nomadic herdsmen who traveled with their flocks seeking ever-changing seasonal pasture land. People also engaged in the cultivation of orchards, growing dates, peaches, apricots, and other fruits, and produced frankincense and myrrh—commodities as valuable in the ancient world as oil is in the modern. An intense devotion to the arts of music and poetry was another characteristic of Arab culture. The religion of these pre-Islamic desert warriors was polytheistic and pantheistic. Insofar as there was a central shrine, it was Mecca, the lively commercial hub of numerous trade routes and home of the Kaaba, in which was housed the sacred Black Stone. This holy object, some seven inches in diameter, was built into the east wall of the Kaaba and was said to have been given to Abraham by an angel. Muhammad taught that it had been pure white when it came to earth but that the sins of mankind turned it black.

During the reign of Omar (r. 634–644), the third Caliph or successor to the Prophet, the entire Arabian peninsula was brought under Muslim control. The desert tribes of Arabia were historically pillagers, but as Islam spread, they were forbidden to steal from fellow Muslims. They therefore turned their sights north to the Palestinian territories controlled by the Christian Roman Empire and the Zoroastrian dominion of Mesopotamia and Iran. Both areas offered little resistance. Each suffered from internal weaknesses that made them appealing targets.

Muslims defeated the Byzantine Greeks in Syria in 634, which became the base for future military conquests. Damascus fell in 635, Antioch in 636, and Jerusalem in 638. Caliph Omar traveled to Jerusalem, where he met the Christian Patriarch Sophronius and exacted an easy tribute. Arab victories in the Palestinian area encouraged a vast wave of immigration from the Arabian peninsula to the new territories. By 641, Muslims controlled all of Syria, Persia, and Egypt.

Fɪɢ. I.10. Caliph Omar in Jerusalem (15th century). Omar displays his progress in the reconstruction of the Temple of Jerusalem to the Patriarch Sophronius.

Spain was invaded in 711, and southern Spain remained under Islamic dominion for five hundred years thereafter. Muslim expansion into France was checked, first by Charles Martel in 732 and again in 759 by Pepin the Short. In Spain, Islamic achievements in art, architecture, and poetry accompanied a generally fair and effective political administration. Muslims introduced scientific agriculture and metallurgy. Cordova in the tenth century was considered the most sophisticated city in Europe, with paved sidewalks, lighted streets, bridges, a large freshwater aqueduct, beautiful gardens, and a renowned university.

Northern Spain was home to the displaced Christians, poor and weak in contrast to the south. Political disunion was fomented by the feudal structure of a weakened king and an independent and aggressive nobility. Agricultural ineptitude kept the people poor and ill fed. The *reconquista* of Spain lasted well into the thirteenth century as Christians fought to expel the Muslims. After a two-century lull in this effort, the Christian conquest of Granada in 1492 ended the political power of Islam in Europe at that time.

Europe's Emergence from the Dark Ages

The medieval view of the approaching millennium was increasingly fraught with anxiety as the tenth century progressed. The Revelation of Saint John had declared the importance of the one-thousand-year period. Interpretations ranged from the eradication of the wicked to the establishment of the reign of Satan, from the second coming of Christ to the destruction of the earth. When the year 1000 came and went rather uneventfully, a sense of anticlimax, even cautious optimism, replaced fear. European Christianity began to awaken to the possibility of options.

Tentative social developments of the mid-tenth century flourished in the eleventh. Frontiers receded as the great forests were cleared and swamps were drained, providing lumber for renewed construction and lands for agriculture. The use of water-powered mills to grind grain and water-powered sawmills to prepare lumber increased the supply of food and shelter. The horse collar and stirrups improved transportation. The widening vistas of emergence from the Dark Ages encouraged increased mobility as nobles, merchants, ecclesiastics, scholars, and pilgrims were willing to brave the dangers posed by both the robber barons in their great castles and the bands of brigands who infested European roads.

Cities grew as centers of commerce and crafts. Merchants and artisans sought to protect themselves by forming guilds and corporations. Rights of self-government were purchased by groups of these wealthy bourgeois who were increasingly able to exert political control of the cities they built. Venice, Genoa, and Pisa became the international commercial centers of western Europe. Navigational improvements encouraged sea trade. Western Europeans began to penetrate the Mediterranean, long controlled by Byzantines and Muslims.

Churches and monasteries were built throughout the eleventh century as the Roman Catholic consolidation of Europe was bearing fruit in increased piety. The popularity of the pilgrimage to the Holy Land as an act of religious devotion became widespread. The devotee could walk in the very footsteps of Christ and the many other heroes and heroines of the Bible. European pilgrims, young and old, rich and poor, traveled in large numbers throughout Europe and the Near East in search of spiritual growth and religious experience.

Jerusalem

Jerusalem was the major destination of the medieval pilgrim. A tax paid to the Muslims enabled Christians to travel safely to the various holy shrines in Palestine. Yet, as the pilgrimage increased in importance in medieval Europe, a growing sense of frustration developed among the faithful against the four and a half centuries of Muslim rule of the Holy Land.

Jerusalem had long been under the control of Europe. Alexander the Great had taken the city in 334 B.C. The region remained under Hellenic dominion until Rome began her conquest in 190 B.C. Jerusalem then became part of the Roman Empire. In 638, the Muslim army took the Holy City, and it had been in their hands ever since. By the eighth century, Arabs predominated in the population.

Jerusalem is as sacred to Islam as it is to Judaism and Christianity. In 691, the Omayyad caliph Abd-al-Malik erected a group of structures known as the Venerable Sanctuary near the site of the Church of the Holy Sepulcher. He built the Dome of the Rock to house the rock viewed by

FIG. I.11. Medieval Jerusalem (15th century). In this imaginative illustration, the Church of the Holy Sepulcher is suggested by the larger gold-domed building to the left, while the Dome of the Rock is the blue-topped building to the right.

FIG. I.12. Jerusalem seen from the Mount of Olives (Steven Brooke). The Dome of the Rock is visible to the right.

FIG. I.13. Mount of Olives (Steven Brooke). A pilgrimage location for both Christians and Jews. Jesus is said to have ascended to Heaven from here. The Garden of Gethsemane is at the foot.

Fig. I.14. The Mount of Temptation at Jericho (Steven Brooke). The site of the forty-day fast of Jesus and his confrontations with Satan described in Matt 4: 1–11.

Fig. I.15. Garden of Gethsemane. (Steven Brooke). Scene of the betrayal and arrest of Christ in Matt 26: 30–57.

FIG. I.16. Church of the Holy Sepulcher (Steven Brooke). Build ca. 336 by St. Helena, mother of Constantine, on the site of the Crucifixion, it is the holiest shrine of Christendom.

FIG. I.17. Scene of the Last Supper (Steven Brooke). Jesus and his Disciples celebrated the Passover feast here. In the twelfth century, it became the Crusader Church of Our Lady of Mt. Zion.

FIG. I.18. Prison of Jesus (Steven Brooke). This chapel is located in the Church of the Holy Sepulcher. Jesus was held prisoner here prior to the Crucifixion.

FIG. I.19. Tomb of the Virgin Mary (Steven Brooke). The Church of St. Mary in the Valley of Jehosophat is venerated as the burial place of the Mother of Christ.

the Jews as the center of the world. It was upon this rock that Abraham was said to have intended to sacrifice Isaac in response to God's command, where Moses received the Ark of the Covenant, and over which Solomon and Herod had built their temples. From this rock Muhammad had ascended to Heaven astride his winged steed; if one had enough faith, the Prophet's footprints were still visible. This rock was also where Muhammad's encounters with Abraham, Moses, and Jesus took place.

EASTERN AND WESTERN CHRISTIANITY

The medieval popularity of the pilgrimage also engendered a fascination, to the point of obses-

sion, with Constantinople and the Byzantine Empire. The Crown of Thorns itself was believed to be in the possession of the Greek Orthodox Church along with other major relics of the Christian faith. The division between the Eastern Orthodox and Western Roman Churches had continued to escalate since the third-century division of the Roman Empire.

During the seventh-century Islamic conquests of Alexandria, Antioch, and Jerusalem, the patriarchs of these regions were displaced. Thus the Patriarch of Constantinople became the true head

FIG. I.20. OPPOSITE: Jesus's Burial Chamber (Steven Brooke). This somber shrine in the Church of the Holy Sepulcher was built over the site of the tomb of Christ.

FIG. I.21. Byzantine emperor Alexius Comnenus (12th century).

of the Eastern Church, as the Roman pope had assumed control of the West.

The division between the Eastern and Western churches continued to intensify. In 1054, the Great Schism finally occurred between Rome and Constantinople. The Greek Orthodox patriarch was officially excommunicated by the Roman pope. Christianity was irreparably divided.

In 1081, Alexius Comnenus came to the throne as Byzantine emperor. He faced a perilous military situation that had been worsened by the Turkish seizure of Jerusalem in 1076. The Turkish forces were now on the march to Constantinople. In 1095, during the Council of Piacenza, Alexius appealed to the Christian West to come to the aid of the Christian East. He offered to join the Eastern to the Western Church in return for Western aid against the Muslims—thus setting the stage for the Crusades.

FIG. I.22. The capture of Jerusalem (14th century). Christ looks on in sorrow as the Saracen infidel marches triumphant into His Holy City in 638.

✠

CHAPTER I

The First Crusade and Victory

The First Crusade was undertaken some twenty-five years before the founding of the Templars. Urban II assumed the papacy in 1088. One of his first acts as pope had been to lift the excommunication of the Byzantine emperor. Representatives of Alexius Comnenus were in attendance at the Council of Piacenza to plead for Western assistance in their decade-long battle against the Seljuk Turks.

Urban could see many benefits to helping the Eastern Church. The opportunity to strengthen Christianity by promoting a greater alliance with Constantinople was certainly alluring. The chance to finally put the many disruptive and warlike knights to a

FIG. 1.1. Pope Urban (14th century). The pope is shown traveling to the Council of Clermont and preaching in favor of the First Crusade.

FIG. 1.2. Peter the Hermit (14th century). The inspired anchorite is shown here at the head of his disastrous Crusade.

killing neighboring Jews in their own communities and along the route. Six months later, after many thousands of Christian deaths, those who had survived were wiped out by the Turks after journeying beyond Constantinople.

The organized armies were slower and more meticulous in their progress, departing in four separate groups between August and October 1096. The first was led by Godfrey de Bouillon, duke of Lower Lorraine, and his younger brother Baldwin. The second army was led by Bohemond, Norman prince of Taranto in Italy, and his nephew Tancred. The third was led by Raymond, count of Toulouse and St. Gilles. The fourth was led by Robert of Normandy, the son of William the Conqueror; Robert of Flanders; and Stephen of Blois, William's son-in-law. Some thirty-five thousand soldiers participated.[1]

useful purpose would be salutary. The possibility that a united Christianity might develop the political will and military capability to eradicate the infidel from the Holy Land appeared to Urban's understanding to be aligned with the divine plan. The merciful God who had allowed humanity to survive the millennium would certainly desire His Church to reclaim Christ's homeland.

Urban traveled through France amid rumors of celestial signs such as the aurora borealis, comets, and star showers. In November 1095 he convened the Council of Clermont and issued his call for the First Crusade. This was one of history's inexplicably perfect moments when an idea can inflame an entire population. Vast numbers heeded Urban's call. Nobles and knights at once began to lay plans for a crusade to begin after the harvest in August 1096. This was too long a wait for the masses. A mob of over twenty thousand souls, led by Peter the Hermit, began the long journey to the Holy Land after first attacking and

FIG. 1.3. The leaders of the First Crusade (19th century). Shown here are Godfrey de Bouillon, Bohemond, Raymond, and Robert of Normandy.

FIG. 1.4. Siege of Nicaea (12th century). The Crusaders are shown flinging severed heads by catapults during this brutal battle in 1097.

The first battle of the Crusades was fought at Nicaea in Turkey. The Turks were overly confident after their effortless victory against the People's Crusade and were defeated by the more disciplined European forces. By the conclusion of this siege, all four Crusader armies had made their rendezvous. They continued a unified march across Turkey, battling the infidel while facing harsh conditions of hunger and thirst. They reached the northern region of Palestine and the city of Antioch in October 1097. (Baldwin's army had separated from the conjoined forces and continued to eastern Turkey, where he succeeded in establishing himself as prince of Edessa.)

The main force laid siege to Antioch. The strength of the city's fortifications, the poor weather conditions, and the lack of food contributed to a long and painful siege. One-seventh of the army died of hunger. Finally, in June 1098, the Crusaders were able to take Antioch. They came into possession of what many

believed to be the Lance that pierced the side of Christ as he hung upon the cross. A meteorite fell from the sky, injuring the Turkish forces. Angels clad in white mantles, carrying a white banner, and mounted on white horses were said to have aided the Christian army.

In June 1099, the Crusaders began the siege of Jerusalem which lasted only five weeks, until Friday, June 15, at midday, the hour of the Crucifixion. A contemporary Crusader reported that soldiers were wading up to their ankles in the blood of the enemy. Urban died just two weeks before Jerusalem was taken. The leaders of the four armies all survived the campaign. Some returned to Europe; others remained and divided the territory in the following manner: Baldwin was established in Edessa; Bohemond became prince of Antioch; Tancred became prince of

FIG. 1.5. The Holy Lance (12th century). The Battle of Antioch brought the return of this precious relic to the armies of Christendom.

Fig. 1.6. The Crusaders take Jerusalem in 1099 (14th century). Soldiers are inspired by visions of the Passion of Christ as they scale the walls of the Holy City.

FIG. 1.7. Godfrey de Bouillon (13th century). The Crusader leader rides off with his army to battle.

Galilee; and Godfrey de Bouillon was elected Advocate of the Holy Sepulcher in Jerusalem. Godfrey felt it wrong to wear a royal crown in the city where Christ had worn the Crown of Thorns and so refused the title of King of Jerusalem.

Godfrey died within a year. His brother Baldwin traveled from Edessa and was crowned King Baldwin I of Jerusalem on November 11, 1100. Baldwin consistently strengthened and extended European power throughout his reign. Upon his death on April 2, 1118, the succession passed in an orderly manner to his cousin, who was crowned as Baldwin II.

CHAPTER **2**

✝

The Knights Templar Order

THE FOUNDING

The Knights Templar, or Poor Knights of the Temple of Solomon, or Poor Fellow-Soldiers of Jesus Christ, were founded by Hughes de Payens, a French knight who had taken religious vows upon the death of his wife. He is known to have been an austere man of deeply held spiritual values, humility, and uncompromising valor. He was nearly fifty when he founded the Order, a veteran of the First Crusade who had spent the previous twenty-two years of his life east of Europe.

Two of the most widespread accounts of the Order's founding agree that in 1118 or 1119, Hughes, along with eight other knights, took vows of obedience to the Patriarch of Jerusalem, resolving to live in holy poverty and chastity, and to devote themselves to the care and protection of Christian pilgrims traveling through the Holy Land. King Baldwin II awarded them lodging in the al-Aqsa mosque near the Dome of the Rock, the original site of the Temple of Solomon.

The timing of the founding of the Knights Templar was critical. A group of seven hundred pilgrims had been attacked on the

FIG. 2.1. Hughes de Payens (19th century). Idealized portrait.

FIG. 2.2. Templar Seal (34 mm). The two knights on the obverse riding on one horse symbolized the Order's embrace of poverty. The reverse depicts the al-Aqsa mosque, the original headquarters of the Knights Templar.

FIG. 2.3. The Dome of the Rock (Steven Brooke). Built in 691 by Caliph Abd-al-Malik, it sits on a location sacred to the three great monotheistic faiths of Judaism, Christianity, and Islam. See text on pages 22 and 28.

eve of Easter 1119. Three hundred were brutally massacred. Sixty more were taken prisoner, and all the possessions of the group were seized as booty. Despair swept through Jerusalem. The establishment of the Order was a prerequisite for the continued survival of Christendom in the Holy Land.

The Hospitallers, or Order of the Hospital of Saint John of Jerusalem (now the Knights of Malta), had been established around 1080 as a charitable group to provide medical care and shelter for pilgrims and had received papal recognition in 1113. During the 1130s, the Hospitallers became involved in military activities, although militarism was never the exclusive province of the Hospital as it was of the Temple.

Jerusalem was virtually isolated from the rest of the European holdings in Palestine. Though symbolically and emotionally of the greatest importance to Crusaders, the city was surrounded by Muslims and in constant danger of attack. It was ruled jointly by the Patriarch of Jerusalem, the Latin king, and whichever particularly powerful crusading feudal lord might be in the area—a politically unstable situation that

FIG. 2.4. OPPOSITE: Interior of the Dome of the Rock (Steven Brooke).

FIG. 2.5. Al-Aqsa Mosque (Steven Brooke). Built 705–715 by Caliph al-Walid, it has been rebuilt several times since.

FIG. 2.6. Interior of al-Aqsa Mosque (Steven Brooke). This is an extremely rare photograph of the original home of the Knights Templar during the Crusades.

FIG. 2.7. Pilgrims traveling by ship (13th century). The harsh conditions of travel by sea during this period became even more dangerous when the Pilgrims reached their destination in the Holy Land.

often led to breakdowns in communication and conflicts of interest.

The dangers to pilgrims were manifold as there was little control of the route between the port of Jaffa (modern Tel Aviv) and Jerusalem, some thirty-five miles as the crow flies—a two-day journey along a dangerous mountain road through fierce desert heat and arid terrain, surrounded by brigands, Muslim armies, and wild animals such as lions. The Holy Land endured a chronic shortage of stable military manpower.

The port cities of Palestine were the only real centers of economic activity. Merchants from the Italian cities of Genoa, Pisa, and Venice conducted a brisk Mediterranean trade. The desire of King Baldwin I to build up the Western population of Jerusalem as a safeguard against the sur-

rounding Muslim enemies motivated him to provide economic incentives to encourage people to move there.

SAINT BERNARD OF CLAIRVAUX AND THE GROWTH OF THE ORDER

The young Order was particularly vulnerable to any number of problems. The knights, having pledged themselves to poverty, wore secular clothing donated by the faithful. Their seal shows two knights riding a single horse, emblematic of the vow of poverty and their humble origins. Their quarters were described as somewhat dilapidated by a contemporary historian. Yet they were growing.

Saint Bernard, who rose to become the most

FIG. 2.8. Bernard of Clairvaux (15th century). The saint is shown preaching to his Cistercian monks above, and triumphing over the temptations of a demon below.

influential and politically powerful Catholic theologian of his time, took a deep interest in the fledgling Order. Bernard was the nephew of André de Montbard, one of the original knights of the Temple and later a Grand Master. Bernard was a member of the Cistercian Order and was chosen to be the first abbot of the Monastery of Clairvaux.

In 1126, André de Montbard and a Templar named Gondemar left Jerusalem for Europe. Baldwin II had written to Bernard, asking for his help in getting papal approval for the Templar Order and crafting a Rule to guide Templar conduct. Hughes de Payens traveled to Europe shortly thereafter to recruit new knights, solicit donations of land and money, and spread the word of the Order's works.

Bernard was of enormous help to the Templars. He was uniquely qualified to synthesize the concept of a knightly religious order. Born in 1090, he had grown up intending to become a knight until he experienced a religious conversion at the age of twenty that forever changed his life. At age thirty-six, Bernard was approaching the height of his power. While chronic ill health made him physically frail, he radiated an immense spiritual vitality. His personal influence on the twelfth-century Church is incalculable by modern standards. He literally functioned as the conscience of Christianity. That which he supported flourished, that which he condemned withered. His energetic support of the Templars practically guaranteed their success.

Bernard had become a Cistercian monk in 1112, when the brotherhood was on the verge of failure. In 1115, at the age of twenty-five, he was chosen to become the superior of Clairvaux. Under his leadership the Cistercians grew from seven abbeys in 1118 to 328 in 1152. He was an extremely talented organizer who had a particular skill for hierarchical organization and the effi-

cient structuring of power. He applied this skill to the Templars.

Bernard was also a highly developed mystic. He was a leading exponent of the cult of the Virgin Mary that began to flourish in the twelfth century. The ideal of the Virgin as mother and intercessor would inform the Templar Order. Bernard realized the tremendous emotional potential offered by the worship of the mother of Christ. He taught that a sincere, ardent, and

Fig. 2.9. Church of Notre Dame des Anges (Vere Chappell).

FIG. 2.10. Council of Troyes (19th century). Official recognition as an established Order of the Church under Pope Honorius was a decisive event in the history of the Templar Order.

sustained aspiration on the part of the seeker would result in a "sweet inpouring of the Divine Love."[1]

In January 1128, the papal council, convened at Bernard's request, assembled at Troyes, some ninety miles southeast of Paris. The purpose of the Council of Troyes was to discuss the Templar question as it had been advanced by Hughes, Baldwin II, and Bernard. Numerous archbishops, bishops, and abbots attended. Pope Honorius II was represented by his legate. At the command of the pope and of Stephen, the Patriarch of Jerusalem, a Rule was written for the Order. The pope also awarded the Templars their own distinctive dress, a plain white robe, to which a red cross would be affixed in 1147.

THE TEMPLAR RULE

Bernard presided over the writing of the original Rule that dictated the behavior of the members of the Order. The Templar Rule was expanded throughout the Order's history.

"We speak firstly to all those who secretly despise their own will and desire with a pure heart to serve the sovereign king as a knight and with studious care desire to wear, and wear permanently, the very noble armour of obedience."[2] In the opening sentences of the Rule, Bernard weaves a tapestry in which he celebrates the ideal of pure knighthood and perfect chivalry and exposes the failing of then-modern secular knights to live up to that high standard. "In this religious order has flourished and is revitalized the order of knighthood. This knighthood despised the love of justice that constitutes its duties and did not do what it should, that is, defend the poor, widows, orphans and churches, but strove to plunder despoil and kill."[3] Edward Burman remarks, "The Templars themselves already looked back to an imagined ideal knight-hood as later sects and secret societies dreamed back to the Templars."[4]

Among the Rule's provisions are the following: The Master of the Order was all-powerful, so powerful that the final paragraph of the Bernard's Rule stated that all the provisions contained therein were to be followed or not at the discretion of the Master. His term of office was for life. His death was celebrated with great dignity and many prayers. His successor was chosen by an electoral college of thirteen members—eight knights and four sergeants representing the twelve apostles, plus a chaplain brother symbolizing Jesus Christ.

FIG. 2.11. Mounted Templars (13th century). Contemporary historian and illustrator Matthew Paris, a Benedictine monk, depicts the two knights riding on one horse shown on the Order seal (see figure 2.2 on page 37) as well as the piebald standard.

The responsibilities of the elite corps of knights were strict. The daily religious lifestyle of the Templar house was based on that of the Benedictine monk, including extensive prayer and attendance at Mass. This was, of course, counterbalanced by the necessity to attend to weapons, armor, horses, and the other tools of the warrior trade. The knights were to wear the white habit at all times except when in the hospital. No decorations were allowed on weapons or armor. They were to say twenty-six Paternosters upon rising and sixty more before eating; in all the prayer was to be repeated 148 times each day. Meals were to be taken together in silence, with neither wine nor water present at the table. Meals were to be accompanied by scripture reading. Leftovers were to be distributed to servants and the poor. One-tenth of all bread was to be given as alms. Meat was allowed three days per week. A light was to burn in Templar dormitories all night.

Templars observed two seasons of Lent each year, at Easter and at Christmas, with forty days of partial fasting prescribed for each. On the other hand, the traditional monastic fast common to religious brotherhoods was forbidden to the Templars, as it was essential they maintain physical fitness for battle. Knights were to wear the tonsure and live amid the simplest of all furnishings as further signs of poverty and humility. The Master, in commemoration of Christ's humility, was obliged to wash the feet of thirteen paupers on Maundy Thursday (the Thursday before Good Friday). He was then to distribute clothing, food, and alms. The knights were also directed to perform this annual ceremonial oblation and almsgiving. Hunting was forbidden, except of lions, identified by Saint Peter as a form of the devil (1 Peter 5:8). All property was held in common. Even a personal letter was to be read aloud in the presence of the Master. Provisions were made for the care of elderly, pensioned, and sick members.

The Order was open to men only. The knights were under strict vows of celibacy and were forbidden to marry or remain married upon

FIG. 2.12. Templars and lion. The proportional representation may suggest the overwhelming power of evil against which the white clad Templars must persevere. On the other hand, the apparent ease of the mien of the Templars may imply a taming of chthonic forces. Yet, note the identification of Christ as "the Lion of the tribe of Judah" in Revelation 5:5.

joining. Wives of men who became Templars were expected to join other religious orders as nuns. Templars were forbidden to kiss their mothers, wives, sisters, or any woman. They were warned against even looking upon women. Knights were forbidden to act as godparents. While the Rule may have had an almost misogynistic quality, it also makes especially clear the role of the Virgin Mary: "Our Lady was the beginning of our Order, and in her and in her honour, if we please God, will be the end of our lives and the end of our Order, whenever God wishes it to be."[5]

Extensive military instructions were an important part of the Rule. Setting up camp and maintaining discipline within the camp were discussed at length. Instructions were given regarding conduct during charges, as well as in battle,

FIG. 2.14. Avignon Cathedral (Vere Chappell). Bernard's celebration of the Divine Feminine was an important development for Christianity.

and included the proper protocols for handling the Order's piebald standard. The hierarchy of discipline in the field was clearly delineated and options in defeat carefully enunciated.

The reception of a brother into the Order is described in detail in the Rule. First the Chapter Master determined that no one present opposed the candidate, who was then told of the harshness of the Templar life. A highly personal interrogation of the candidate's character and life history next took place. He was questioned as to his willingness to give up his former life and surrender himself to a life of service to the Order.

FIG. 2.15. St. Benedict (11th century). The Templar Rule was patterned after that of the fourth century monastery at Monte Cassino founded by Benedict.

FIG. 2.15. Two Templars at chess (13th century). From a book on chess produced for Alfonzo X, king of Léon and Castile. Compare with figure 15.6 on page 176 where a Templar plays chess with a Muslim.

Each new member heard the secret Rule read for the first time at his ceremony of initiation. He was required to swear an oath of absolute obedience and loyalty to the Master and to the Rule, to take vows of poverty and chastity, and to swear to capture and defend Jerusalem. Finally, he was given instructions regarding the disciplines he was to follow for the rest of his life. The ceremony of reception as described in the Rule has no indication of the behavior charged by the fourteenth-century Inquisition.[6]

Punishment for infractions against the Rule ranged from lesser humiliations such as being forced to eat from the floor for as long as a year and a day, or the loss of one's habit and all privileges and responsibilities of knighthood, or expulsion from the Order, to the possibility of perpetual imprisonment. In 1301, the Master of Ireland, William Le Bachelor, was excommunicated and starved to death in a tiny cell overlooking the church. His crime was selling Templar land without permission. From his cell, he could observe the Mass and the brethren taking part in the Communion from which he was excluded.

Weekly chapter meetings were held in Templar houses in which four or more brothers lived. After a sermon, the floor was opened to brothers who wished to confess violations of the Rule. Punishment would be assigned by the chapter acting in concert while the brother left the room so the discussion could be private. Accusations might take the place of confession during these sessions. If the guilt of those accused was proven, offenders were punished more severely than those who voluntarily confessed. Accusations were later made by the Order's enemies that this self-policing practice was intended to be the equivalent of the sacrament of penance, which required a priest. While this was not true, some of the simpler-minded brethren were unclear on the issue. A reading of the Rule can help us to understand their confusion.

The Rule states that no brother was supposed to confess to anyone but a chaplain brother, "for they have greater power to absolve them on behalf of the pope than an archbishop."[7] Yet chaplain brothers were not able to absolve certain specific sins: killing a Christian; striking a brother so that blood flows; laying a hand on a man of another order whether clerk or priest; renouncing one's vows to another order upon joining the Templars; or becoming a Templar through simony. These sins could only be absolved by the local patriarch, archbishop, or bishop.

Initially nine offenses merited expulsion from the Order. These were simony; disclosing the secrets of a chapter; killing a Christian man or woman; theft; leaving the house other than by the gate (which implied thievery or other sinister motive); conspiracy between brothers; treason with the Saracens; heresy; and fleeing the raised piebald standard during battle from fear of the enemy. "[T]he filthy stinking sin of sodomy"[8] was later added as an expellable offense, as was entering the Order as a layman and taking ordination without the permission of the house.

IN PRAISE OF THE NEW KNIGHTHOOD

Bernard made another contribution of vast importance to the Order's recruiting efforts and subsequent myth. Bernard wrote a long letter to Hughes in which he expounded in detail on his

FIG. 2.16. The Fall of Simon Magus (12th century). In Acts of the Apostles 8:9–24, the magician Simon seeks to purchase spiritual power from the apostles, thereby giving his name to the sacrilege of bartering material value for religious virtue.

views of the code of chivalry and his concept of the ideal of the holy knight. The treatise was entitled *Liber ad milites Templi: De laude novae militae*, "The Book of the Knights of the Temple: In Praise of the New Knighthood," and is believed to have been written in 1135.

The letter was designed to be a guide for current and future members of the Order; to encourage prospective members to apply for admission; and to provide a rationale for the Order within the context of Christianity. It was also an answer to those critics who believed Christianity had no place for an armed brotherhood of warrior-monks whose dual goals of salvation and soldiering were said to be mutually exclusive.

Bernard harshly criticized the vanity and pompousness of secular knights with their flowing hair, silks and jewels, plumed armor, and painted shields, calling them "the trinkets of a woman."[9] The new knighthood "is one that is unknown by the ages. They fight two wars, one against adversaries of flesh and blood, and another against a spiritual army of wickedness in the heavens."[10] The knight-monk is a soldier of Christ. "Neither does he bear the sword in vain, for he is God's minister for the punishment of evildoers and for the praise of the good. If he kills an evildoer, he is not a mankiller, but, if I may so put it, a killer of evil."[11] The essential religious justification for the slaying of the enemies of Christ by so respected a theologian as Bernard established the concept above the reach of criticism.

The primary quality for which the Templars were long to be known, in addition to their discipline, was their courage. The Muslims respected them for this as much as the Europeans did. Despite frequent losses over the next two hundred years, Templar courage was rarely questioned. Roots of this may certainly be traced to

Bernard's exhortations in *De laude:* "Truly, he is a fearless knight and completely secure. While his body is properly armed for these circumstances, his soul is also clothed with the armor of faith. He fears neither demons, nor men. . . . "[12] "On the exterior, steel, not gold, is their security—since they are to strike fear in the enemy, not provoke his avariciousness. They need to have horses that are swift and strong, not pompous and decorated. Their purpose is fighting, not parades. They seek victory, not glory. They would rather strike terror than impress. . . . "[13]

THE STRUCTURE OF THE ORDER

The knights were, of course, the prime element of the Order. The bulk of the Rule applied to their conduct. There was no actual training program for knights. One was expected to be a fully functional warrior upon joining. Knights were drawn exclusively from the nobility. The actual percentage of knights within the overall membership of

FIG. 2.17. Sir Geoffrey Luttrell (14th century). This secular knight appears to embody the precise values St. Bernard criticized in his seminal missive to Hughes de Payens. Luttrell is shown preparing to set off for a tournament, attended by his wife and daughter-in-law. The rude virtues Bernard preached to the Templars were a perfect foil to the vanity and self-indulgence of the day.

FIG. 2.18. The Defeat of Satan's Army (13th century). The medieval warrior felt no need for relativistic paroxysms of conscience or multicultural appreciation for the enemy's point-of-view. The Muslims were regarded as Satan's spawn. Bernard made clear that here was a battle between Good and Evil, both in Heaven and upon Earth.

the Temple was always quite small after its earliest beginnings. It is estimated by various historians that ten percent is the most reasonable figure. It is estimated that the size of the Order just prior to its downfall was fifteen thousand members, of whom ten percent were knights.[14] The knights were the only members entitled to wear the celebrated white robe and red cross.

The bulk of the members, quite literally a supporting army, were charged with administering the vast requirements of the elite core of heavily armed and mounted knights. The sergeants

were the ranking members of this elaborate logistical system. Their duties included everything from cooking to warfare. Their uniforms were a black tunic with a red cross on the front and back and a black or brown mantle. The sergeants were entrusted with responsibilities often equal in scope to that of the knights, despite their lesser status. They would be in full charge of running the Templar household when the knights were away.

Numerous serving brothers functioned in various capacities such as foot soldiers, clergy,

FIG. 2.19. King David slays the Amalekites (13th century). The identification of the crusading armies with the ancient Israelites is illustrated in this biblical battle scene. The depiction of the ancient combatants wearing then-modern medieval clothing, weapons, and armor is fascinating.

recruiters, armorers, blacksmiths, grooms, cooks, brewers, tanners, engineers, masons, carpenters, architects, medical personnel, servants, and laborers. The care of horses was one of the most important activities. Vast resources and energy were required to ship, house, feed, and maintain the equine army. (Each knight was allowed to possess up to three horses.) A large number of Templars administered the finances of the Order as it grew to be one of the wealthiest institutions of medieval Europe. Others were charged with maintenance and administration of the vast tracts of land donated to the Order. Templar farms required experts in agriculture and animal husbandry as well as field hands. A distribution apparatus for produce, wool, meat, and other products developed over time. Donated lands might be let out for rental income, and facilities

such as mills, wine presses, and mines also served as sources of income. In later years, the Templars became involved in shipping, developing their own fleets to move pilgrims, soldiers, and supplies along the Mediterranean route to the Holy Land, which naturally expanded to include trade. Templar houses were maintained in key port cities.

The purpose of these varied activities was to raise the funds and materials necessary for the campaign in the Holy Land. The vast European support network was one of the most important accomplishments of the Order. Without it, the Templars would have ceased to exist after their first major defeat. The European supply base of money, goods, and manpower kept the Order alive through two centuries of continual warfare.

TEMPLAR FINANCIAL INNOVATIONS

The Knights Templar established the practice of international banking. Their numerous fortresses along the routes leading eastward naturally suggested themselves as depositories for gold and other valuables to kings, nobles, merchants, crusaders, and pilgrims. It was safer to trust the Templar network for monetary transfers than to carry large sums of cash along dangerous routes. Funds deposited with the Order in Europe could be claimed on arrival in the Holy Land as needed. The paper records between Templars in various locations establishing these deposits and pay-

FIG. 2.20. Logistics of the Crusades (13th century). Here, a young David delivers provisions prior to a battle. It is illustrative of both the supplying of the crusader armies, and the psychological identification of the Crusaders with biblical roots.

ments ultimately led to the modern practice of drawing checks against an account.

Those about to embark on the years-long and dangerous journey abroad would often make up wills and leave these safely in the hands of the Templars. Thus the Order might be required to fulfill the fiduciary duties of executor for estates left in their care. The Templars were also frequently the recipients of grants of large amounts of cash. In some cases, the money would be specifically earmarked for a crusading purpose. In other cases, the money would be donated as a gift to the Order. Record keeping had to be precise.

As time went on, the financial skills developed by the Order became even more sophisticated. In France especially, the Templar financial bureaucracy was utilized to perform extensive banking services for the monarchy. These activities included assessing and collecting taxes, transmitting funds, managing debt and credit, and

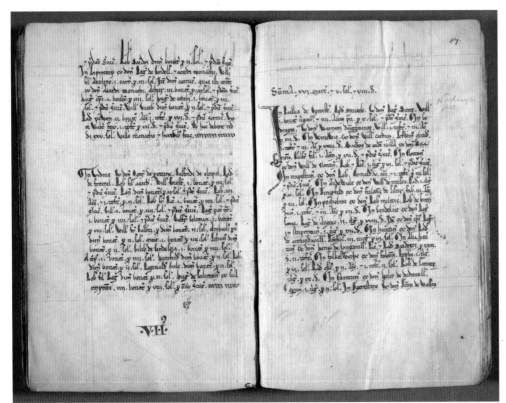

FIG. 2.21. Templar Inquest Book of 1185. The extent and variety of Templar holdings demanded strict accounting. This is the record of an audit conducted by the Master of the English Temple of the Order's holdings throughout the country.

paying pensions. The nobility, encouraged by the confidence shown by royalty, made similar use of the brothers.

The armed security offered by the well-guarded Templar houses was so impressive that they were used to hold deposits of royal treasure in England as early as 1185. The crown jewels were deposited in the London Temple in 1204. Templar depositories were also used to hold funds in escrow accounts for contractual guarantees among parties. In addition to valuables such as gold, jewels, and documents, livestock and even slaves are known to have been entrusted to Templar safekeeping in Aragon.[15] Again, superior record keeping was necessary to the success they enjoyed, as was a proper and trustworthy assaying bureaucracy capable of accurately establishing the value of deposited goods.

The overall European Templar network was instrumental in contributing to the development of a cash-based economy for the first time in Europe. For example, Templar farms originated the practice of raising crops for sale. Before this, farming was practiced for the sustenance of those who provided the land and/or labor. The constant demand for funds to pursue the crusading effort forced the Templars to become financial innovators. The Holy Land already functioned primarily as a cash economy. Disposable wealth counted for more than property, which was vulnerable to the constantly changing strategic situation. The Templars were able to adapt to this circumstance. Familiarity with the workings of a cash economy gave the Order the experience that would place it at the vanguard as the European economy gradually shifted itself in this direction.

The medieval prohibition against usury was carefully skirted by sophisticated forms of contracts. Interest payments were concealed as administrative expenses, deducted in advance

FIG. 2.22. Society as composed of three mutually supportive orders (13th century). The Templar organization uniquely represented the evolving social ideal of the eleventh century in which those who till the earth, those who fight, and those who pray join their efforts to achieve the larger goal.

from the moneys received by the borrower or achieved through careful manipulation of the exchange rates of foreign currencies. Money lending by the Templars dated back to the Order's earliest days under Hughes de Payens, who perceived it as one of the duties of the Order—in spite of the fact that Bernard was virulently opposed to materialism and the money trade in general. Almost all European monarchs had occasion to borrow from the Templars, as did several monasteries.

Although the Templars were wealthy in both land and hard assets, the fabulous wealth often ascribed to the Order is undoubtedly an exaggeration. The enormous costs associated with conducting a two-hundred-year military campaign must be factored into the myth of their extraordinary wealth. Funds were constantly required for the normal expenses associated with equipping, transporting, housing, and feeding the vast number of personnel involved. In addition, castle construction, maintenance, and rebuilding were huge financial drains, as were the large sums paid in ransom, lost in unrepaid loans, and seized by the enemy in battle.

✠

CHAPTER 3

The Growth of the Knights Templar

THE RISE OF THE TEMPLARS IN EUROPE

The support of Bernard, papal recognition in the form of the Rule, and the status conferred by the Council of Troyes all contributed to an increase in membership in the Order. The promise of glory, danger, travel, religious expiation, and the chance to fight to establish God's kingdom on earth fell upon waiting and ready ears. The concept of a military-religious order of knight-monks was an idea whose time had come. Within a short period of time the Templars began to amass stores of wealth and land donated by aristocrats excited by their charisma and seeking remission of sins through acts of generosity to a holy order of the Church. Hughes de Payens was one of the first to donate his own lands. France was naturally the first area of expansion, as the prime participants were native to the country. Hughes soon appointed a National Master of the Temple for France, thus laying the foundation for an international bureaucratic structure.

He next visited England and Scotland, where he also received donations of land, money, and volunteers. He established the London Temple in 1128 or 1129. The English branch of the Order prospered greatly under King Stephen, who ascended to the throne in 1135. Stephen's father had participated in the First Crusade, and his wife was the niece of King Baldwin I of Jerusalem. Exemption from the heavy layers of English taxation proved enormously helpful to the growth of the English Temple.

In 1130, the Order was established on the Spanish peninsula, the scene of the first Templar military campaign against the Moors. The Templars of Aragon were uniquely required to swear an oath of loyalty to the king in addition to their oaths to the Order. Under the patronage of the rulers of Catalonia and Aragon, they received large land grants in recognition of the value of their military support. In neighboring Portugal, Queen Theresa donated a castle and surrounding land.

FIG. 3.1. Chateau Royale (Vere Chappell). This castle in the Mediterranean town of Colliure, France was built by the Templars.
FIG. 3.2. Sainte Eulalie de Cernon (Vere Chappell). The most important Templar Commandery in Southern France.

Fig. 3.3. OPPOSITE ABOVE: La Couvertoirade (Vere Chappell). Walled town built by the Templars.

Fig. 3.4. OPPOSITE BELOW LEFT: La Couvertoirade (Vere Chappell).

Fig. 3.5. OPPOSITE BELOW RIGHT: Templar Church at Sainte Eutalie de Cernon (Vere Chappell).

Fig. 3.6. ABOVE: Another view of the Chateau Royale in Colliure (Vere Chappell).

FIG. 3.7. Shipley Chapel in Sussex (Photo by Dame Stella Bernardi). This was one of the largest Templar preceptories in England.

FIG. 3.8. Sompting Tower, also in Sussex (Photo by Dame Stella Bernardi).

The growth of the Order was slower in Italy because of the fragmented political organization of that country. Italy, however, did have a number of port cities along its coast from which Crusaders, merchants, and pilgrims embarked to the Holy Land. The Order established a presence in each of these.

GROWTH IN THE HOLY LAND

In 1129, Count Fulk, an early friend of the Templars, accompanied Hughes de Payens on his return to Palestine (which came to be known as *Outremer,* "Beyond the Sea"). Baldwin II, who had no male heir, had offered Fulk the hand of his eldest daughter, Melissande, in an attempt to cement the lineage of the kingdom of Jerusalem. Fulk and Hughes traveled with as many as three hundred new members who would serve in the Holy Land. Other new members from Hughes's successful recruitment campaign remained in Europe. Payen de Montdidier, the Master of France, was entrusted with overseeing all Euro-

pean Templar activities. Many of the new volunteers made substantial contributions of material wealth to the Order upon their renunciation of secular life.

Fulk and Melissande were married at the end of May 1129. Baldwin immediately enlisted Fulk and the newly enlarged Templar force in his plan to attack Damascus. The battle took place in October. The Christians were thoroughly beaten. The inexperience of the recently arrived European recruits contributed to the clumsiness of the Templar efforts. The defeat, however, did not lessen their prestige either in the Holy Land or in Europe. Reports of Templar bravery traveled home with secular knights and returning pilgrims. A conference took place in Toulouse whose purpose was to confer gifts upon the Order. Forty-five donors contributed money and property. The Order's fame, wealth, and membership continued to grow.

The ongoing success of the Templar's recruiting efforts was particularly welcome at this time. The rise of the Muslim warrior Zangi—a former

FIG. 3.9. The Templar Church in London (Photo by Dame Stella Bernardi). This chapel served the
English Templars since 1161. It was consecrated in 1185 by Heraclius, Patriarch of Jerusalem.
After the aboliton of the Order in 1312, King Edward II turned it over to the Hospitallers.

FIG. 3.10. An illumination from the *Book of Psalms of Queen Melissande* (12th century). This is the only surviving manuscript known to have been created in the Holy Land at this time.

FIG. 3.11. The siege of Shayzar (13th century).
A combined force attacked this stronghold belonging to
Zangi in 1132. The Byzantine emperor John Comnenus
(son of Alexius) was joined by the armies of Raymond
of Antioch and Joscelin of Edessa. The siege was lifted
after three weeks when a large ransom was paid to
the Crusaders.

Kurdish slave of the Seljuk sultan Malikshah who
went on to found the Atabeg dynasty—was cor-
rectly perceived as a particularly threatening
development to Christian interests. In 1128 Zangi
became governor of Aleppo, and by 1130 he was
the master of northern Syria.

When Prince Bohemond of Antioch was
killed in battle in 1130, his widow Alice,
youngest daughter of Baldwin II, declared herself
regent of Antioch and offered her allegiance to
Zangi. This was an intolerable situation for Baldwin. He and Fulk immediately intervened and
Alice was banished. Baldwin again became regent
of Antioch, a position he had gladly relinquished
to Bohemond and Alice in 1126.

Baldwin II died in August 1131. Fulk and
Mellissande succeeded him, crowned together in

FIG. 3.12. Zangi (Paul Kirchner). An idealized portrait of
one of the greatest Muslim commanders of the Crusades.

FIG. 3.13. Baghras Castle (David Nicolle). Located in the Amanus Mountains in the northernmost reaches of the Crusader states, Baghras was among the first possessions of the fledgling Order.

September. Alice soon returned to Antioch to plague them. Fulk managed to subdue a threatened rebellion. In 1136, he craftily contrived a marriage between Alice's nine-year-old daughter Constance and Raymond of Poitiers. Raymond's presence added strength once again to the region as he and Fulk were able to function as a united Christian front.

There is little record of Templar activity during the 1130s. They were undoubtedly engaged in integrating new members and building the training programs needed to transform European knights into soldiers capable of dealing with the varied tactics and strategies they would encounter in their new environment. The enormous and sudden increase in Templar numbers created

other practical and logistical demands that would require full attention to accommodate successfully. The Order was given its first group of castles along the northernmost frontier of the Holy Land, the Amanus Mountains, either by Fulk in 1131 or by Raymond in 1136.

As the European presence in the Holy Land continued, the Order's original goal of protecting pilgrims assumed less importance. The Knights Templar increasingly evolved into a crusading fighting force. The Muslims followed battle tactics entirely different from those commonly employed by European soldiers, and as a result, several early military actions ended in unmitigated disaster for the Europeans. The firsthand, hard-won experience the Templars were to gain

Fig. 3.14. Abu Ghosh (Steven Brooke). This Church, built in 1141 some 10 miles west of Jerusalem, is one of the earliest Crusader constructions.

from their military encounters with the Muslims would recommend them as strategic advisors to the kings and nobles who came to fight their season in the Holy Land.

Hughes de Payens died on May 24, 1136. The Order he founded was successfully established and would become an eternal mythic component of Western civilization. The deaths of Hughes and Baldwin II heralded the end of the first generation of Crusaders.

"EVERY BEST GIFT" AND PAPAL SUPPORT

Innocent II became pope in 1130 and was a major advocate for the Templars. He granted the Order an annual papal tribute. Other clerics enlarged upon this from their own resources. In 1138, he met with Templar Grand Master Robert de Craon, an intelligent and persuasive diplomat. De Craon carefully explained the financial and administrative burdens facing the Order as it expanded to fill the ever-increasing needs of the campaigns in the Holy Land. Innocent listened carefully. He understood that the Church must maintain the physical muscle to protect its spiritual mission.

On March 29, 1139, Innocent II issued the fundamental papal bull on the Templars, *Omne datum optimum*, "Every best gift." Bernard was in Rome at the time and must have rejoiced. This landmark edict proclaimed the Templars as the "true Israelites" who followed the precepts of spiritual charity and divine love. The bull created a new category of chaplain brother, or priest, within the Order to minister to the spiritual welfare of knights and serving brothers throughout

FIG. 3.15. St. Peter's Basilica in Rome (Steven Brooke). Christ said, "Thou art Peter, and upon this rock I will build my church." (Matt 16:18). Rebuilt during the Renaissance, this church is the center of Roman Catholicism.

FIG. 3.16. Interior of St. Peter's (Steven Brooke). This masterpiece of Renaissance architecture is a monument to the power of the religious instinct in mankind and rivals the great temples of Ancient Egypt in its grandeur.

the widespread houses of the Order, thus freeing the Templars of all local ecclesiastical authority. The Order was responsible to the pope alone. The Templars were his private army; he their sole authority. They were granted the right to construct their own churches to protect themselves from the company of sinners. They were allowed to retain any booty seized in battle. They were exempted from all church tithes and authorized to collect tithes for themselves. They were freed from all authority except that of the pope. This included kings and emperors as well as the entire church hierarchy. No one was permitted to require an oath of a Templar. No one who was

not already a Templar could be elected as Master of the Order (making it more difficult for a king to "fix" an election). All changes to the Rule were to be made only by the Master and a chapter of knights. Furthermore, the bull not only identified the Templars as protectors of pilgrims en route to Jerusalem but asserted that God and Saint Peter had authorized them to protect the Catholic Church itself and to defend it against enemies of the Cross.

Omne datum optimum was frequently repeated by succeeding popes who further strengthened the Order with later bulls. In 1144, Celestine II issued *Milites Templi*, which awarded

indulgences to benefactors of the Templars. It also granted permission to supporters to hold collections for the Order once a year in churches. It allowed for the celebration of Mass in areas under interdiction when Templar collectors were present. Pope Eugenius III, a disciple of Bernard's, issued *Milites Dei* in 1145, which authorized a change in battle-standard design from the rectangular piebald battle standard to an eight-pointed black Maltese cross on a plain white background. *Milites Dei* further gave the Order permission to build chapels independent of diocesan authority and to bury Templar dead in graveyards attached to these independent chapels.[1] *Omne datum optimum, Milites Templi,* and *Milites Dei* quelled any moral doubt about the Templar mission in orthodox Catholic thought. The holy warrior, who wielded his weapons of destruction in the establishment and protection of Christ's kingdom on earth, was to be aided and abetted by all, loved and respected, and showered with material gifts.

FIG. 3.17. Templar Knight (Richard Scollins). This contemporary illustration shows the original Templar white robe with the famed red cross added by Pope Eugenius in 1147. *Milites Dei* replaced the Piebald Standard shown here with a black Maltese cross on a white background.

CHAPTER 4

✝

The Second Crusade and the Syrian Assassins

The decade beginning in 1130 represented a turning point in the history of Outremer. The European occupation would require more sophisticated organizational strategies to remain viable after the loss of the initial emotional fervor that followed in the wake of the victory of the First Crusade. While that fervor was rekindled by the meteoric success of the Templar recruiting efforts, the politics of the Holy Land had become very complex indeed. The European inhabitants, collectively known as the Franks, were divided into four separate Crusader states: the kingdom of Jerusalem, the principality of Antioch, the county of Tripoli, and the short-lived county of Edessa. These states were often in conflict with each other.

The decentralization of the Muslims and their own conflicting centers of power further contributed to the instability and fluidity of the political situation. Various temporary alliances and arrangements were made with one or another ruler or group as seemed useful. Land and castles changed hands frequently, both through conquest and by treaty. Sometimes enemies, plotting against each other, allied across religious and cultural lines to attack their coreligionists.

THE ASSASSINS (NIZARI ISMAILIS)

One Muslim group that was to play a large role in the Templar story was the Order of Assassins. More properly called the Nizari Ismailis, they were founded by Hasan-i-Sabah, a Persian adept, who reigned at the mountain fortress known as Alamut from 1090 to 1124. Based on a complex theory of the proper succession within the bloodline of the prophet Muhammad, the Assassins, under the leadership of the Aga Khan, remain a vibrant and important Muslin sect to this day. At the beginning of their military phase, which lasted approximately 150 years,

FIG. 4.1. Hasan-i-Sabah (18th century). Idealized portrait.

FIG. 4.2. The Garden of Delights at Alamut (14th century). In this rare image, Hasan-i-Sabah is shown supervising the administering of the magic potion prior to admitting the Assassin disciples (the *fidais*) to the Garden.

Hasan developed the use of assassination as a political tool by which his community was able to successfully alter the balance of power in a hostile region. Soon after securing Alamut, he sent Nizari missionaries, known as *dais,* many thousands of miles away to Aleppo to build a Syrian branch of the Order.

In the beginning of the fourteenth century, Marco Polo fueled the European fascination with the Assassins when he described legends of a magnificent enclosed garden hidden at Alamut in which all details corresponded to Muhammad's description of Paradise: it contained every variety of fruit, gilded pavilions, exquisite paintings, and silk tapestries. Wine, milk, honey, and water freely flowed throughout. Beautiful women skilled in music, singing, dancing, and the arts of love attended to the every wish of those who were chosen to enter its guarded walls, for the garden was impregnable.

The only people allowed to enter were young disciples, carefully chosen for their martial prowess and personal loyalty to the Assassin leader, "the Old Man of the Mountain." He would first give them a drugged potion that would cause them to enter a deep sleep. They would awaken to find themselves within the magic garden. These simple youths would spend a period of time in blissful sensuality until the potion was again administered and they would awaken at the castle. Once conducted to the Old Man's presence, they would discuss the experience with the Master. He would then assign one of them a target for assassination. The chosen youth would be promised that upon his return and successful completion of the task he would be readmitted to the garden, or should he die during the mission, the Old Man would send his angels to bear the young man's soul to Paradise.[1]

While there is absolutely no evidence for this

intriguing fantasy, the word *assassin* entered nearly all medieval European languages to describe a hired or political killer. European popular culture embraced the quality of the disciples' loyalty to the Old Man. Medieval troubadours promised their loved ones the same devotion as the Assassin held toward his mysterious Master. Gradually fear of Assassin skill and cunning spread within the royal courts of European monarchs. Kings suspected enemies of forging murderous alliances with the Old Man, who would then send his dark minions against them.

It was Hasan-i-Sabah's early mission to the Ismailis of Syria that resulted in the early European contact with the Assassins during the Crusades. The mythical Old Man of the Mountain,

celebrated by troubadours and feared by kings, was the Syrian chief of the Order.

The first documented contact between the Assassins and the Crusaders took place in September 1106. Tancred, prince of Antioch, attacked the newly acquired Nizari castle of Apace outside of Aleppo. The Christians defeated the Assassins and leveled a tribute against the sect. Tancred forced the Syrian chief of the Order to ransom himself. In 1110, the Nizaris lost a second piece of territory to Tancred.

Despite these losses, the Syrian Assassins were able to help in expelling Crusader troops from various strongholds, a feat that other Muslim leaders had been unable to accomplish. In 1125, under the leadership of the next Syrian chief, Bahram, Nizari soldiers provided critically needed military support against the Franks. The Damascene ruler Tughitigin gave the Assassins the frontier fortress of Baniyas, which they began to fortify and use as their base to send out missionaries and conduct military operations throughout Syria.

FIG. 4.3. The assassination of Nizam al-Mulk (14th century). Nizam was the chief advisor to the Seljuk sultan Malikshah. His death in 1092 at the hand of Bu Tahir Arrani, a *fidai* sent by Hasan-i-Sabah, helped lift a deadly siege against the Assassin headquarters at Alamut.

FIG. 4.4. Muslims and Christians in battle (14th century). The opposing armies during the Crusades were both possessed of the certainty that their mission was the will of God. Yet they called that God by different names.

In 1128, after Tughitigin's death, an anti-Ismaili wave arose in Damascus which resulted in a general massacre of some six thousand Ismailis. Rumor spread that the Assassins had made an alliance with the Franks to betray Damascus in return for Tyre. While this was untrue, Bahram's successor, al-Ajami, had written to Baldwin II, king of Jerusalem, with an offer to surrender Baniyas in exchange for safe haven from his Sunni persecutors. Al-Ajami died in exile among the Franks in 1130.

In 1140 the Assassins took the important fortress at Masyaf. In 1142, the Hospitallers received the nearby castle of Krak des Chevaliers.

In 1149, the Assassins cooperated with Raymond of Antioch in an unsuccessful battle against the Turkish Zangids, during which both Raymond and the Assassin leader Alf ibn Wafa were killed. The alliance with Raymond was motivated by Nizari perception of Raymond's strength against the Zangids who had just taken Aleppo.

The shifting alliances of the period are well illustrated by the fact that in 1151, the Assassins battled the Franks over Maniqa, and in 1152 they assassinated their first Frankish victim, Count Raymond II of Tripoli. This shocking murder led to a Templar attack against the Nizaris and the imposition of an annual tribute of some two thousand gold pieces payable to the Templars.

The interreligious hostilities and shifting alliances of Outremer were hardly limited to the Assassins. The Seljuks (representing the Abbasids), Fatimids, and Omayyads were three competing Muslim dynasties engaged in constant power struggles with one another. All were severally engaged in hostilities with the Assassins. Alliances such as that between the Damascene sultan and King Fulk against Zangi in 1139 would have been incomprehensible to the medieval European unfamiliar with the harsh diplomatic realities of the Holy Land. The Templars were faced with a complex web of intrigue that often defied the simple idealism inherent in their founding—and would later return to haunt them with accusations of treason.

Among Christians, disunity was equally pronounced. The Byzantines had a long-standing financial relationship with the Muslim states that preceded the Crusades. Their Islamic business interests and alliances were of a more permanent and practical nature than those formed by the inflamed passions of the Crusades. In addition, the Greeks understood that if the European power in the Holy Land was encouraged to grow unchecked, it could rival and surpass their own.

The alliance between the Roman and Byzantine Christians burst apart in 1137. During the First Crusade, an agreement had been made between the Eastern emperor and the crusading armies. The Franks would receive the full support of the emperor if they agreed that any captured Muslim land that had previously belonged to the Byzantines would be returned. Antioch was one such territory, yet it had remained in Frankish hands since 1098. In 1137, Emperor John Comnenus laid siege to Antioch. Christian battled Christian. Worse, King Fulk of Jerusalem refused to assist Prince Raymond of Antioch

despite their alliance. Thus Antioch became a Byzantine territory again, and Raymond was forced to pay homage to the emperor.

In the midst of all this, in 1144 the county of Edessa was taken after a four-week siege by Zangi. This development buoyed up the Muslims with enthusiasm and self-confidence, while it left Europe with a sense of despair and anger. It marked the first great Christian defeat since the victory of the First Crusade fifty years before. Pope Eugenius III immediately began to call for a new crusade. He chose the French King Louis VII as the leader of the mission. Bernard of Clairvaux was passionately involved in preaching for the Second Crusade. He began in France in 1146 and traveled widely through Europe, everywhere

FIG. 4.5. St. Bernard preaching the Second Crusade in company with King Louis VII (Detail, 15th century).

exhorting the crowds to action. This was to be the largest of the Crusades; it included French, German, English, and Italian troops. Military actions were also fought against the remaining Moors in Spain and the Wends in Germany.

Louis VII, Bernard, and Pope Eugenius, accompanied by some three hundred Knights Templar and four archbishops, gathered at a Templar chapter meeting in Paris in 1147 to inaugurate the Second Crusade. Louis was presented with the *oriflamme*, a scarlet banner emblazoned with a golden flame and mounted upon a golden lance. Eugenius granted the Templars the exclusive right to wear a red cross upon the left breast and shoulder of their mantles, thus adding the red badge of martyrdom to the white robe of purity.[2]

Everard des Barres, the Templar National Master of France, participated as one of three ambassadors in a successful diplomatic mission to the Byzantine emperor to negotiate a peaceful passage for the French army. He also joined in intimate sessions with Louis, arranging for the necessities of the Crusaders. The Templars fought

Fig. 4.6. The Templar Chapter meeting of April 22, 1147 in Paris (19th century). This convocation represented the official launching of the Second Crusade.

and behaved admirably and with great dignity during the hazardous journey from Constantinople across Asia Minor to Antioch. During the long march, they reaffirmed their reputation as warriors and served as moral examples of loyalty and courage to the European troops. The French force was a motley crew, composed of assorted groups of soldiers loyal to various

nobles who were often rivals of each other. Adding to the confusion was the presence of the German army under King Conrad III. The combined forces lacked a common language, let alone overall coordination and cohesion. This contrasted with the iron discipline of the Templars inspired by their Rule. King Louis eventually placed the Templars in command of all the troops. In 1148, each soldier took an oath that he would obey Templar instructions.

During the Second Crusade, the Templars made a historic loan to Louis. The king had spent much more money than expected on supplies and shipping during the journey to Antioch. By the time the army arrived in March 1148, he was in severe need of funds, which could only be repaid upon his return to France. The Templars were able to come to his assistance. From this point on, the Knights Templar became an essential component of any European plan or campaign undertaken in the Holy Land.

In June 1148, the Templars gathered near Acre with the Hospitallers, King Baldwin, the Patriarch of Jerusalem, Kings Louis and Conrad, the archbishops of Caesarea and Nazareth, and other local nobles and church officials. It was decided to attack Damascus. A force of fifty thousand Christians laid siege to the city but failed to attain victory. A series of tactical errors caused the great army to disintegrate within five days. Rumors and accusations of treason, bribery, and treachery were made against various leaders. Blame was laid at the feet of the European kings, who were accused of ambition and stupidity for choosing to attack the friendly Damascenes. The Palestinian barons were accused of committing treason out of jealousy for the initial successes of the visiting kings or in return for a bribe paid by the Damascenes. The Templars were also accused of accepting enemy bribes to set up the army for failure.

The Second Crusade was a blistering defeat for Europe. A great deal of resentment was directed toward the Byzantines. Their treacherous alliances with the Turks had caused much loss of life for the European forces as they marched overland to Antioch. Louis left Palestine calling for a crusade to be launched against the Byzantines. Bernard, bitterly disappointed by the failure of the Second Crusade, lent his support to a Byzantine Crusade. Everard des Barres, who succeeded Robert de Craon as Grand Master, accompanied Louis to France to help plan the new crusade. Christian was preparing to go to war against Christian.

The brothers in Outremer, however, faced a perilous new situation. Zangi had died in 1146 while his army laid siege to Damascus. His son and successor, Nur al-Din, defeated a Frankish army and killed Prince Raymond in a battle near Antioch. The Templars attempted to help Baldwin III, who rushed to fight Nur al-Din, but most of the Templar force was killed by the Islamic army. André de Montbard, Seneschal of the Order, wrote Everard imploring him to return after alerting Europe to the seriousness of the new developments. Everard did return in 1152 but soon resigned as Grand Master to become a monk under Bernard at Clairvaux.

The Templars succeeded in securing a military base at Gaza, ten miles south of Ascalon. The Fatimid stronghold at Ascalon had been a continuous menace to the kingdom of Jerusalem since the First Crusade. From Gaza, the Templars launched repeated swift attacks against Ascalon

FIG. 4.7. The Siege of Damascus by Kings Louis VII of France and Conrad of Germany (13th century). Resentments and recriminations followed the lack of success of this effort.

Fɪɢ. 4.8. The ruins of the Castle of Ascalon (Steven Brooke). This Mediterranean stronghold served as a trade route and strategic doorway between Egypt, Palestine, and Mesopotamia for millennia.

in imitation of Muslim tactics. Their success with this strategy greatly altered the balance of power in the southern region of the Holy Land.

Ascalon, however, was to be the scene of one of the worst accusations of cupidity made against the Templars. A long siege against the city was undertaken in January 1153 by the army of the kingdom of Jerusalem. On August 15, a breach was opened in a wall near a Templar camp. The new Grand Master, Bernard de Tremelay, reportedly refused to allow any other troops to enter the breach so that the Order alone could reap the first spoils. This act of apparent greed resulted in the Master's death along with that of thirty-nine of his knights. The Muslims soon sealed the breach, and the forty Templar corpses were hung

Fɪɢ. 4.9. Nur al-Din (Paul Kirchner). The son of Zangi, this Muslim general appears to have inherited his father's tactical brilliance and courage.

77

from the castle the next morning, while their heads were sent as trophies to the caliph in Cairo. Ascalon fell a week later, but the Templars were denied any credit for the victory or share in the copious booty.

Bernard of Clairvaux died on August 20, 1153. Pope Eugenius died the same year. André de Montbard became the fifth Master of the Temple. In 1154, Nur al-Din fulfilled his father's dream by taking Damascus. The idea of a Byzantine crusade lay dormant.

Another interesting contemporary story sheds further light on the complexity of the Templar situation and the controversy that swirled about them. In 1153 and 1154, a power struggle in Cairo resulted in the murder of the caliph. The powerful vizier, who had arranged the murder, planned to elevate his son to the throne. However, the coup failed and father and son were forced to flee with much treasure. Captured by the Templars near Ascalon, their wealth was confiscated, the father killed, and the son imprisoned. Despite his professed willingness to convert to Christianity, the Templars sold the young man back to the Egyptians, who promptly murdered him. It is unknown whether the Templars acted out of greed, a natural distrust of the sincerity of the enemy, or from a legitimate desire to increase their wealth to be able to more effectively fight in the name of their faith. A similar incident in 1172 involving the alleged willingness of the Assassins to convert to Christianity is discussed on page 82.

FIG. 4.10. Saracen baptism (14th century). The Templars were more interested in killing the enemy than in converting him to Christianity.

CHAPTER 5

✛

The Rise of Saladin

The mid–twelfth century witnessed the development of an important new trend among the Franks. Secular lords began to donate castles to the military orders and to rely on the orders to defend the territories included in these grants. The baronage realized that the cost of maintaining sufficient troops and supplies was simply too high; it was cheaper to contribute excess property to the military orders than to be forced to defend it. It has been estimated that by the time of the Battle of Hattin in 1187, the Templars and Hospitallers held about thirty-five percent of the lordships in Outremer.[1] The military orders were thus becoming independent factors in the political equation of the region— sometimes at odds with each other, sometimes at odds with the

FIG. 5.1. Chastel Blanc [Safita] (David Nicolle). Located in the principality of Tripoli, near Tortosa, this strategic castle remained in Order hands from the first half of the twelfth century until it was conquered by Baybars in 1271.

barons. Political fragmentation and rivalry among the Christians thereby increased.

In 1162, the throne of Jerusalem passed to Amalric, a powerful leader who, like his rival Nur al-Din, recognized the strategic importance of Egypt. If Egypt were in Islamic hands, the Europeans would be totally surrounded. If it were in Frankish hands, the Muslims would remain permanently splintered. Amalric attacked the Fatimids in Egypt in 1164 and again in 1167. Nur al-Din sent his Kurdish general, Shirkuh, against Egypt in 1164 and 1167. Although Amalric was repulsed both times, his second campaign resulted in a mutually favorable treaty with the Fatimids, who sought his aid against Shirkuh. When Amalric proposed a third assault on Egypt in 1168, in violation of his treaty, the Templars refused to support him. They claimed it would be dishonorable for the king to break his word. Amalric proceeded without the Templars and was defeated.

Enemies of the Order claimed they had violated their mission to defend the kingdom of Jerusalem. Yet even William of Tyre, one of their harshest critics of the day, believed they acted honorably in this instance. A practical consideration influencing their decision may have been the incredible financial drain of the disastrous Second Crusade. Templar resources were also strained by their efforts to protect their northern fortresses from Nur al-Din. The Hospitallers were in the midst of a major financial crisis from which they hoped the Egyptian campaign might provide relief. Instead, it worsened their situation to such a degree that the Master of the Hospital resigned in disgrace. Another Templar motivation may have been lingering resentment against Amalric for his actions against a small garrison that had surrendered to Shirkuh in 1166. Amalric had rushed to reinforce them but arrived too late. In his fury, he decided the Templars had not put up

sufficient resistance and executed twelve men by hanging.

Shirkuh was the uncle of the legendary Muslim leader Saladin, "Righteousness of the Faith," who would one day be responsible for the singular accomplishment of uniting the numerous Islamic factions. Saladin was born in 1138 in Syria, east of Beirut, and died in Damascus in 1193. Saladin's father, Ayyub, was the governor of Baalbek under Zangi, and then of Damascus under Nur al-Din. Saladin grew up following the pursuits of a young nobleman. He studied the Koran, Arabic poetry, and philosophy. He became expert in hunting, riding, chess, and polo. Saladin's martial prowess was developed as he fought in Shirkuh's campaigns. During the battles against Amalric in 1167, Saladin was given his first command. He managed to withstand a seventy-five-day siege by the Christian army. In 1171, he launched an attack against Amalric from Egypt.

Shirkuh took the office of vizier, or sultan, under the Fatimid caliph al-Adid in Cairo in 1169. Upon the death of Shirkuh, Saladin assumed his uncle's position. Within two years, he overthrew the caliph and became the ruler of Egypt. After two and a half centuries, Ismailism ceased to be the state religion, as Saladin returned Egypt to the Sunni fold. Upon the death of Nur al-Din in 1174, Saladin had himself crowned as the first king of the Ayyubid dynasty. He believed he was destined to be the leader of the jihad against the European infidel. A man of simple tastes, he died with barely enough money to pay for his funeral. Yet he routed the infidel, and his tomb in Damascus is to this day a pilgrimage site. Saladin was considered by friend and foe alike to possess the universally respected virtues of justice, courage, fairness, faithfulness, and piety. He never broke a treaty.

Saladin was involved in a unique rivalry with

FIG. 5.2. Saladin (12th century). The greatest proponent of Muslim unity since the Prophet himself, Saladin (1137–1193) was esteemed by friend and foe alike as an embodiment of the principles of Chivalry.

the Syrian Assassin Master Rashid al-Din Sinan. The quintessential Old Man of the Mountain, Sinan reigned from 1162 to 1192. The Syrian Nizaris were in a precarious position because of the immediacy of the Crusader invasion and the ascension of Saladin to the Egyptian throne. Saladin dreamed of a single Islamic society governed by the purest religious principles. Both Nur al-Din and Saladin regarded the Frankish Christians as their most dangerous enemies but viewed the Assassins as dangerous heretics of deep concern.

Sinan, therefore, faced a complex situation that called for cultivating a successful relationship with the Crusaders, with whom he, as a Muslim, was technically at war. The Assassins were already paying a tribute to the Templars by

the time he took charge. In 1173, he sent an ambassador to King Amalric I of Jerusalem proposing an alliance against Saladin. Their sole condition was that Amalric lift an annual tribute of some two thousand gold pieces they had been paying to the Templars for two decades. Amalric promised the Templars he would make up for any financial loss they might suffer and sent the Assassin ambassador back to Sinan with his message. During his return journey, the ambassador was murdered by a Templar knight named Walter de Mesnil. The recently elevated Templar Grand Master was the fiery-tempered Odo de Saint-Amand. It is not known if Odo ordered the slaying, but he did support Walter. Amalric demanded Walter be turned over to him and

FIG. 5.3. Rashid al-Din Sinan (Paul Kirchner). Sinan reigned as the Master of the Syrian Assassins from 1162–1192. He was a charismatic and powerful leader. Statesman, mystic, warrior, and adept, he was feared as the Old Man of the Mountain—by whose command enemies were neutralized by the dagger of the *fidai*—yet he remains one of the most venerated figures in Nizari Ismaili history.

tried. Odo refused, invoking the privileges extended to the Order by *Omne datum optimum*. Amalric, enraged, burst into the house where Walter was staying, arrested him, and threw him into prison. Walter henceforth disappeared from the historical record. The possibility of an alliance with the Assassins was lost. Any potential for additional discussion was negated by Amalric's death soon after in 1174.

Archbishop William of Tyre, a contemporary historian, wrote that Sinan had expressed, through his ambassador, the willingness of the

Assassins to convert to Christianity in furtherance of such an alliance. Modern Ismaili scholars dismiss this as a gross misinterpretation of Sinan's offer and claim the sophistication of Sinan's theological interests and his ecumenical viewpoint would naturally incline him to learn more of the religious doctrines of his potential allies.[2]

Sinan next unsuccessfully tried to assassinate Saladin in 1175 and again in 1176. In August 1176, Saladin laid siege to the Assassin headquarters at Masyaf. Then, without warning, he ended the siege and departed. Various explanations have been given, including the following account from Sinan's biographer. One day a messenger from Sinan approached Saladin. He stated that the message was personal and must be delivered only in privacy. Saladin progressively emptied his court until only two Mameluke attendants were left. Sinan's messenger asked Saladin why he would not order the Mamelukes to depart so he could deliver his message in private. Saladin replied, "I regard these two as my own sons. They and I are one." The messenger then turned to the Mamelukes and said, "If I ordered you in the name of my Master to kill this Sultan, would you do so?" They drew their swords together and replied, "Command us as you wish."[3] This incident seems to have henceforth allied the two leaders. There are no more records of conflict between Saladin and Sinan.

Sinan was a nearly mythological religious figure among the Syrian Nizaris. He had no bodyguards to protect him, ruling through the sheer force of his personality. He traveled from fortress to fortress, with no permanent base or established bureaucracy. Because of his continual movement, the network of Ismaili fortresses was both close-knit and ever alert. William of Tyre, writing during Sinan's reign, estimates that there were some sixty thousand Syrian followers of the

Assassin chief. Sinan was described by another historian as a tender and gentle ruler.

The Templars came under an increasing barrage of criticism as Saladin's victories mounted. In 1160, Pope Alexander III, a strong supporter of the Order, issued a bull forbidding people to pull Templars from their horses, obviously in response to anti-Templar sentiments. King Amalric intended to express his concerns about the growing power and arrogance of the Order to other Christian leaders; however, his death prevented this. In 1175, Pope Alexander III criticized the Order for the burial of excommunicated persons in Templar cemeteries. In 1179, the Third Lateran Council condemned the Templar abuse of the privileges granted by earlier popes. The ecclesiastic leaders demanded the return of all recently acquired churches and tithes, later defined

to mean within ten years of the council. While these demands were never satisfied, they indicate a turn of emotion against the Order.

Saladin laid siege to Damascus in 1174, but the city was rescued with the assistance of the Franks. Yet nothing could prevent him from assuming the leadership of Islam. In 1177, he seized Ascalon with an army of twenty-six thousand men. Here, he received his most humiliating defeat from the combined forces of the Templars and Baldwin IV at Mont Gisard. His opportunity for revenge came shortly thereafter, however,

FIG. 5.4. The army of Saladin (14th century). These fierce warriors inflicted the worst defeats on the Crusader armies of any Muslim force until the final confrontation with the fearsome Baybars and his Mameluke troops a century later.

FIG. 5.5. Renart the Fox attended by the Templar and Hospitaller Grand Masters (13th century). This illustration from the satirical novel *Renart le Nouvel*, 1289, may have carried a more sinister overtone. The reputation of the military orders suffered at each new loss. Antagonism grew at each new privilege. By 1307, the French king was able to accuse the Templars of alliance with the Devil and crush these once great warriors whose entire reason for existence had been the defense of the Christian faith.

when he took the castle of Le Chastellet near Jacob's Ford in 1180. The castle had just been completed the previous year. It was built to block one of Saladin's major military routes. His first attack against the castle failed, but he defeated the Christian army assembled against him at Marj Ayun. Odo de Saint-Amand was taken prisoner and died in a Damascene dungeon in 1181. Saladin sent sappers to dig underneath the outer walls of Le Chastellet to weaken the castle's foundation. When the walls collapsed, the Muslim army attacked. The Templars lost eighty knights and seven hundred fifty sergeants in the battle. Saladin captured seven hundred prisoners and dismantled the castle down to the last stone.

The death of the young Syrian king in 1182 finally allowed Saladin to assume the throne of Damascus. He had thus overcome the last element of fragmented Sunni power and was able to take the title "Sultan of Islam and the Muslims." The Crusaders now faced a united enemy, commanded by a single leader whose sole purpose was their eradication in the name of Allah.

Disunity among the Crusaders fed directly into Saladin's ambitions. For example, when he invaded Tripoli, the Templars possessed one castle in the area and the Hospitallers another. The orders had recently settled a dispute between themselves over territory. Each was so concerned about protecting its own property that the knights remained inside their castles as Saladin's army passed by. Count Raymond of Tripoli was unwilling to engage in a major battle alone against Saladin. Thus, while three separate Christian armies were in immediate proximity, Saladin's force was able to move unmolested through the area, setting fire to harvests, stealing cattle, and killing civilians.

One small, if pathetic, display of unified Frankish behavior occurred in 1184, when the Grand Masters of the Templars and Hospitallers accompanied the Patriarch of Jerusalem on a mission to Italy, France, and England to warn Europe of the dangers of Saladin and to plead for economic and military assistance.

A new crisis over succession to the throne of Jerusalem, however, was about to plunge Outremer into even worse conditions of factionalism, approaching civil war. King Baldwin IV suffered from what was believed to be leprosy. As

he became weaker, he appointed his brother-in-law Guy de Lusignan to rule the kingdom and lead the army. Guy's authority was supported by the Templars and their new Grand Master, Gérard de Ridefort, as well as by other Crusaders. An opposing camp supported Baldwin's cousin, Count Raymond III of Tripoli. When Baldwin died in 1185 at the age of twenty-four, Raymond was chosen as regent for Baldwin's nephew and successor, Baldwin V. The boy king died at the age of ten, however, and Guy de Lusignan immediately seized the throne and proclaimed himself king of Jerusalem.

Saladin was able to take diplomatic and military advantage of the intractable inter-Christian hostilities. For example, the Byzantine emperor made a treaty with Saladin in 1185 in which he promised not to come to the assistance of the Europeans. Count Raymond was also driven into Muslim arms by Gérard de Ridefort, who held a long-standing personal hatred of Raymond. De Ridefort attempted to convince King Guy to attack Raymond and force him to accept Guy's claim to the throne. In response, Raymond made a treaty with Saladin in 1187 in which Saladin promised to make Raymond "King of all the Franks."[4] While this could reasonably be perceived as treason, at least by King Guy, Raymond made no attempt to conceal his actions.

Guy sent a mission to Raymond to attempt to enlist him in a combined effort against Saladin's forthcoming attack. De Ridefort, one of Guy's ambassadors, originally intended the mission to be a military assault on Raymond. But Guy was dissuaded from this course by the other members of the group. As the men were traveling to meet Raymond, a scene was occurring that would soon lead to tragedy. Raymond, following the terms of his treaty with Saladin, had granted safe passage across his lands to a

FIG. 5.6. The Horns of Hattin. It was upon this field that the West suffered one of its most crushing defeats at the hands of the Muslim army under Saladin.

Muslim reconnaissance force of seven thousand soldiers led by Saladin's son, al-Afdal. The permission extended for twenty-four hours. Surrounding villages were alerted and the inhabitants told to remain safely within their dwellings.

When Guy's representatives arrived at Tripoli, de Ridefort learned of the Muslim reconnaissance mission and was determined to attack al-Afdal's army. He made this decision despite the fact that the combined Christian force numbered only some 140 knights, including ninety Templars. The objections of the other leaders to this foolhardy and ill-planned effort served only to fuel Gérard's determination. He prevailed, and on May 1, 1187, the Templars lost eighty-seven knights, including the third-ranking Marshal of

the Temple. Gérard himself escaped but was badly wounded, and the Master of the Hospitallers was killed. Gérard's attitude was not incompatible with Bernard's rhapsodizing on Templar courage in *De laude:* "They rush in to attack the adversaries, considering them like sheep. No matter how outnumbered they do not consider the savage barbarians as formidable multitudes. Not that they are secure in their own abilities, but they trust in the virtue of the Lord Sabaoth to bring them to victory.... We have seen one man in hot pursuit put a thousand to flight and two drive away ten thousand."[5]

This catastrophe further exacerbated the hatred between Gérard and Raymond. On the other hand, Raymond voluntarily submitted himself to Guy in guilty acknowledgment of the disastrous consequences of his treaty with Saladin. The Muslims were encouraged by their bloody victory and prepared for a full-scale attack on the kingdom of Jerusalem.

The decisive Battle of Hattin occurred just over a month later. (The plain of Hattin is located approximately sixty-five miles north of Jerusalem and twenty miles east of Acre.) Saladin had amassed an army of twelve thousand knights against King Guy's force of twelve hundred knights and about fifteen thousand foot soldiers and light cavalry. The animosity between Raymond and Gérard was again to result in disaster for the Christians.

Gérard prevailed on Guy to attack Saladin despite Raymond's objection. Raymond insisted the army should remain where it was, though his wife was trapped at Tiberias, where she had been

FIG. 5.7. The Battle of Hattin (13th century). Matthew Paris chronicles this battle in his *Chronica majora*.

defending their castle. Raymond knew the summer heat could be used to Frankish advantage if they would simply outwait Saladin and allow his troops to be weakened by the oppressive weather. Most of the men present agreed that Raymond was right. Gérard, however, railed impetuously against this view. He called Raymond a traitor because of his unwillingness to break the treaty with Saladin weeks earlier. He mocked Raymond's attitude toward his wife's predicament and called him a coward. He claimed the Templars would be forced to put aside their white mantles and pawn their possessions in shame if they failed to avenge their recent defeat at Saladin's hands. Guy sided with Gérard.

The Christian army therefore left its campsite, a well-watered meadow, to march through a fierce desert. Saladin's army had made camp in another meadow near the Horns of Hattin. On July 4, 1187, the Christian army was decimated. Although the Templars fought valiantly, Saladin took full advantage of the weakness of

FIG. 5.8. The Battle of Hattin (15th century). The magnitude of the campaign at Hattin is communicated by the medieval artist.

the strategic position of the Franks. Thousands were killed. Thousands more were captured. The Muslims took the royal tent and the True Cross. Some two hundred surviving Templar and Hospitaller knights were beheaded. (While it was the medieval practice to ransom captives, Saladin made exceptions of the military orders because of their warlike nature and threat to Islam.) Two hundred thirty Templars died at Hattin, either in battle or by execution. Gérard de Ridefort lived but was imprisoned along with King Guy and a group of barons to be ransomed.

The entire Palestinian region had been left unguarded by the general Christian mobilization in preparation for the Battle of Hattin; few troops remained in place to defend their positions. Within two months, Saladin took Acre, Nablus, Jaffa, Toron, Sidon, Beirut, and Ascalon.

He laid a twelve-day siege against Jerusalem, which fell to the Muslim army on October 2, 1187. Saladin immediately ordered the city cleansed of the hated Christian presence. He had the great cross removed from the Dome of the Rock. The cross was paraded through the streets for two days while it was beaten with sticks. This was the prelude to purifying the mosques with rosewater and restoring them to their pristine condition. Yet Saladin also demonstrated his legendary chivalry by freeing the twenty thousand Christian civilians who had survived the siege. Seven thousand were ransomed with money taken from the treasuries of the military orders; the balance were simply set free. Native Christians were allowed to remain in the city. Ten Hospitaller brothers were permitted to stay in the Order's house, where they could treat the sick for one year.

During the next year, Saladin continued his victories. In a two-year campaign, he had reclaimed the Holy Land. The military orders had been crushed. The remaining Christian territory was reduced to areas along the Mediterranean coast, including Tyre and Tripoli, a castle at Beaufort, and a few other scattered castles. Saladin allowed Bohemond, former ruler of the principality of Antioch, to retain the city of Antioch and one castle.

FIG. 5.9. The Church of St. Anne in Jerusalem (Steven Brooke). Celebrated as the birthplace of the Virgin Mary as early as the third century, this church was destroyed by the Persians in 614. It was rebuilt by the Crusaders in 1140. In 1192, Saladin converted it to a Muslim *madrassa* or religious school. Today it is a Christian monastery.

Fig. 6.1. Sarcophagus of the legendary Crusader king, Richard I, the Lionhearted (13th century).

CHAPTER **6**

✠

The Third Crusade
and Richard the Lionhearted

The defeat at Hattin and the subsequent territorial losses were a defining experience for the Frankish community as they entered the last decade of the twelfth century. The Palestinian Templars were broken men. Their Grand Master remained in Saladin's prison; their numbers were severely reduced; they had lost the respect of others; their pride was shattered.

In Europe, Pope Gregory VIII sent emissaries to all European kings to enlist support for a Third Crusade. His call was enthusiastically received. First to respond was the Holy Roman Emperor Frederick Barbarossa, who left Europe with an army of one hundred thousand men in 1189. After a series of difficulties on the journey, he died by drowning in Armenia, and his army disintegrated. Meanwhile, Kings Philip Augustus of France and Richard I of England prepared for their departures.

A number of European nobles arrived in the Holy Land during the summer of 1189. Many were crammed together within the walls of Tyre where they quarreled among themselves. They were divided between those loyal to King Guy, which included the Templars, and those who supported his rival, the newly arrived Conrad of Montferrat. Guy's power base had been weakened by his imprisonment and bad judgment in listening to Gérard de Ridefort. He had been ransomed from Saladin's prison in July 1188. Conrad, a powerful German marquis, had arrived in Outremer to fulfill his crusading vow in 1188. The fortuitous timing of his arrival, combined with his military prowess, saved Tyre from Muslim conquest. The majority of barons in the city supported him as their natural leader. He established a legitimate claim to the throne of Jerusalem by marrying Isabel, daughter of Amalric.

The conflict with Conrad led Guy and his Templar supporters to a decision to attack the Muslim-controlled city of Acre so that Guy might have a territory in which to exert his full authority.

Fig. 6.2. King Richard I of England and King Philip Augustus of France enter Acre in 1191.

Fig. 6.3. The Capture of Acre in 1191 (ca. 14th century). Defeated Muslim defenders hold up their hands seeking mercy from the conquering Crusader army.

They began the siege in August 1189. Saladin came to the defense of Acre and the Franks unsuccessfully attacked him. Among the thousands of casualties was Gérard de Ridefort. He had recently managed to ransom himself by ordering the Templars to surrender their castle at Gaza. The strategic loss of this "doorway" from Egypt to Palestine must have seemed to many a high price to pay for Gérard's life.

The main force of the Christian army was able to continue the siege of Acre despite the lost battle. They would remain there for two years. In the meantime, King Richard had set out from England, and King Philip sailed from France.

FIG. 6.4. Richard and Saladin (14th century). The clash of the titans as illustrated in the Luttrell Psalter. (See also figure 2.17 on page 50.)

They traveled by separate routes. Richard attacked Cyprus on the way and took possession of the island. He continued his journey, reaching Acre on June 8, 1191. Philip Augustus had just arrived. The two monarchs assisted the wearied army in taking the city on July 12, 1191. Richard ordered the slaughter of his Muslim prisoners during the final battle. In sight of Saladin, his men slew twenty-seven hundred prisoners. Richard's reasons for this uncharacteristic brutality are unclear.

Philip Augustus, largely uninterested in crusading, left for Europe within three weeks of the victory at Acre. King Richard remained. His subsequent activities in the Holy Land gradually helped rebuild the Templar reputation and self-image. Richard decided to sell Cyprus and offered favorable terms to his friend Robert de Sablé, the new Templar Grand Master. Templar ownership of the island would prove an unfortunate experience. They were forced to put down an armed rebellion engendered by their mistreatment of the population and disposed of the island within the year.

In September 1191, with Templar tactical advice to guide him, Richard defeated Saladin at

Arsuf in a brilliantly executed battle strategy. He thereby demonstrated to Christian and Muslim alike that Saladin was not invincible. Shortly after this battle, Richard offered his sister in marriage to al-Adil, Saladin's brother, in an attempt to create a treaty with Saladin. Richard proposed they corule Jerusalem and that Saladin return some properties taken from the military orders. Saladin refused the offer. Richard spent a year battling fiercely against him. Richard's army arrived within sight of Jerusalem, but they sadly turned back without reclaiming it for Christendom. Richard was persuaded by the wisdom of the Templars, Hospitallers, and native barons of the futility of conquering the isolated city. He understood that Jerusalem would be impossible to defend once he and his army returned to Europe. Instead the Franks decided to rebuild Ascalon as a barrier against the free passage of Saladin's armies from Egypt, which helped to compensate for the loss of Gaza.

Richard, meanwhile, was receiving regular reports from England of the treachery of his brother John, who was attempting to take advantage of his absence to seize the throne. Richard was forced to prepare for his return. He therefore inserted himself deeply into the politics of the region.

Some historians suggest Richard may have contracted with the Assassins to slay Conrad of

Montferrat in 1192. Two Assassins disguised as Christian monks were responsible for Conrad's murder. Others believe that Sinan may have ordered Conrad's death because of a request from Saladin. The simplest explanation, however, may be that there had been problems between the Assassins and the Franks during the previous several years. Conrad's recent seizure of a Nizari ship and its cargo, and his murder of the crew, could of themselves have been sufficient motivation for Sinan's vengeance.

Richard arranged for his nephew Henry, count of Champagne, to marry Conrad's widow Isabel within days of Conrad's death, and thus to supplant Guy de Lusignan as king of Jerusalem. Henry was also the nephew of Philip of France, so he was an ideal choice to encourage continued European allegiance to the needs of Outremer.

The death of Conrad also aided Richard in his efforts to conclude a truce with Saladin. They signed a five-year peace treaty in September 1192. The treaty returned cities south of Jaffa to Christian control and opened a safe passage to pilgrims visiting Jerusalem. The Assassins were included in the treaty at Saladin's request. The Templars sold Cyprus to Guy de Lusignan, which conveniently removed him from the region and that troublesome piece of real estate from their concerns. Richard set off for England in October 1192 disguised as a Templar. Thus began an arduous and adventure-filled two-year journey during which he was captured and imprisoned by the German emperor Henry VI, from whom he was ransomed before returning to England.

Saladin died in 1193, a particularly welcome event for Crusaders. Islam fragmented once again, Saladin's hopes for the leadership of his own Ayyubid dynasty notwithstanding. Outremer had managed to survive to enter the new century. Thanks to Richard's treaty, the Franks were able quietly to rebuild while the attention of both Islam and Europe was focused elsewhere. The Templars had experienced a renewal through their contact with the legendary King Richard the Lionhearted.

An interesting tale is told of King Henry and his meeting with the Assassin chief. After his ascension to the throne of Jerusalem, Henry was approached by the Assassins to negotiate an accord. He described his visit, around 1194, to the headquarters of the Old Man of the Mountain in the Nosairi Mountains. Henry and the Master were strolling through the grounds when the Old Man said that he did not believe the Christians were as loyal to their leaders as his disciples were to him. To illustrate his point, he signaled to two youths high above on one of the towers; both immediately leapt to their deaths on the rocks a thousand feet below.

✝

CHAPTER 7

The Byzantine Crusade

The accession of Pope Innocent III in 1198 was another source of good fortune for the Templars. He was a powerful and influential leader who would reign for eighteen years. He maintained an iron will toward establishing the Church as the supreme ruler of a theocratic feudal hierarchy, in which all Christian kings would willingly submit themselves to the authority of the pope. Innocent lavished his protection on the Templars, pointedly reminding the clergy of exemptions and special privileges in matters of financial and religious independence awarded the Order in the past. Yet, he ruled the Templars with an equally firm hand, upbraiding them in a letter in 1207 for their pride and greed and for abusing the grants with which they had been endowed. He

Fig. 7.1. Pope Innocent III (14th century). Innocent is shown excommunicating the Albigensians. After the disastrous failure of the Fourth Crusade, he launched a domestic crusade against this gnostic sect in southern France (see chapter eight).

criticized the practice of granting membership and burial privileges to excommunicated nobles in return for money. He bade them reform themselves. The Knights Templar became Innocent's personal army, the militia of Christ, by which the pope would enforce his will and attain his goals. Among these goals was the liberation of Jerusalem and the elimination of Catharism in Europe.

In 1202, Innocent preached a Fourth Crusade whose glory would equal that of the first. Egypt would be the initial target. Innocent hoped to avoid what he perceived to be the mistakes of

the Second Crusade, when the multinational forces experienced crippling language barriers and the rivalry between proud kings doomed the efforts of Christendom. The army of the Fourth Crusade was led by various nobles deemed loyal to Innocent, of whom Boniface of Montferrat, brother of Conrad, was the overall leader. The Templars helped fund the European armies as they assembled and began to travel east. The plan called for the Palestinian Templars to meet and reinforce the Crusaders upon their arrival in Egypt. They would thus form a united and powerful Christian force. However, this was not to be.

Merchants of the city of Venice had been enlisted to provide the required ships and passage arrangements for the army as well as a year's supply of food. The Crusaders were not aware that the Venetians had made a simultaneous trade agreement with the sultan of Egypt, promising him that no European army would land in the

FIG. 7.2. The Surrender of Zara in 1202 (16th century). The treachery and double dealing of the Venetian merchants and their leader turned the Fourth Crusade into an unmitigated disaster for Christianity. Innocent excommunicated the Crusader armies for their attack against the Christian city of Zara, made at the behest of the Venetians.

FIG. 7.3. The Crusaders take Constantinople (19th century). The wily Venetians took advantage
of long standing resentments against the Byzantine Orthodox Church. The violence of brother
against brother perhaps best describes the vicious looting and pillage that accompanied the
catastrophic "success" of the Fourth Crusade, pitting Roman against Greek Christians
without ever once setting foot on Muslim ground.

territory of Egypt. The Venetians demanded of the Crusaders a price for their services that exceeded the available resources of the leaders of the nearly thirty thousand assembled troops. Then the Venetians proposed a deal. If the Crusaders would capture the Dalmatian port of Zara for Venice, the Venetians would extend credit to them for the balance owed. Although Zara was a Christian city, the Crusaders agreed, and within five days delivered the city to the Venetians. Innocent was mortified at the shedding of Christian blood and excommunicated both the entire city of Venice and the crusading army. Soon after, realizing the army had been manipulated, he lifted the excommunication against them.

Next, the Venetian leader Enrico Dandelo—who maintained a long-standing grudge against Constantinople—suggested the conquest of that city as a detour of opportunity for the Crusaders. They could stamp out the Byzantine heresy and unite all Christendom under the pope; they could avenge the Byzantine treachery of the Second Crusade; and they could avail themselves of the legendary wealth of Constantinople to pay their Venetian debt. The Crusader leaders agreed and attacked Constantinople in 1204. Wholesale looting and pillage followed, inevitably accompanied by drunkenness, sacrilege, murder, and rape. Thousands were killed. Innocent's dream of a united Christianity was destroyed. The Fourth Crusade extinguished itself without ever reaching the infidel. The Latin kingdom of Constantinople established by the Fourth Crusade fell back into Greek hands within sixty years.

The opening of new campaign fronts in the Byzantine Empire and Cyprus was welcomed by many as a new arena for European knights. Now, one who sought the glory and opportunities for wealth and expiation afforded by battle—but who shunned the difficulties of travel to the distant and alien culture of Palestine—had his burden considerably reduced. As a result, since the beginning of the thirteenth century, the military orders composed the virtually exclusive European military presence in the Holy Land.

CHAPTER 8

✠

The Albigensian Heresy

Innocent's disappointment and horror at the sack of Constantinople may have contributed to the fervor with which he pursued his next major military objective, the Albigensian Crusade. Beginning in 1209, this bloody war against heresy lasted for twenty years, ultimately giving birth to the Inquisition. Its victims were the peaceful Cathars of the Languedoc region of France, whose primary center of activity was near the city of Albi. The Cathars were dualist Christians whose antipapist reformist teachings enraged the Church hierarchy. Throughout the Dark Ages, Europe had remained relatively unconcerned with heresy. By the sixth century, material conditions were too harsh to allow for much focus on philosophy during the next four or five centuries. In the eleventh century, however, Manichaean dualism rose again to challenge the exclusive religious hegemony of the Church.

St. Augustine, who founded the first Christian monastic order in 388, had been a member of a Manichaean sect for nine years prior to his conversion. He is responsible for introducing the accusation that licentious sexual practices took place among the Manichaean elect, who, he said, consumed a eucharist of which human sperm was an ingredient. In the early years of the eleventh century, the soon-to-be common tale emerged of a heretical group who chanted demonic names until the evil spirit entered the room. The heretics then extinguished the lights and engaged in an indiscriminate orgy. The ashes of a baby conceived during such an orgy were mixed with excrement and consumed as a eucharist of Hell by the demoniacs. According to historian Malcolm Lambert, the name *Cathar* (often attributed to Greek or Latin roots meaning "cleansing" or "pure") probably comes from the word *cat*.[1] Twelfth-century enemies of the Cathars believed their rites included ritually kissing the anus of a cat, in which form Lucifer was said to appear. Toward the end of the twelfth-century, the Cathars were also slandered by the term *bougre*, from "Bulgaria,"

FIG. 8.1. Interior of the Church of Mary Magdalene, Rennes le Chateau (Vere Chappell). With the Albigensian Crusade, we encounter the terrors of the Inquisition and its battle against heresy. The war against religious error would flame again a century later when the Templars were accused of demonic intercourse and Satanism, and the Order crushed under the weight of those inflammatory charges.

FIG. 8.2. The Pope's private chapel (Steven Brooke). One can imagine Innocent's hours of torment over the manifold errors of the Fourth Crusade and the decision to attack the peaceful Cathars. This is an extremely rare photograph of the Pontiff's personal prayer chapel in St. Peter's. It was, of course, built during the Renaissance, well after Innocent's papacy.

known to be the source of their heresy. Later the word came to mean "sodomite" and is the root of the British slang *bugger* and *buggery*.

As late as 1233, the Roman Catholic Church offered its decisive definition of the Cathar heresy when Pope Gregory IX issued his bull *Vox in Rama*. Here he denounced Cathar worship of Satan and purported to describe their beliefs and practices. He stated that Cathars believed God had erred in casting out Lucifer from Heaven and

that Lucifer would return in triumph to reward his faithful. He described the course of an initiation ceremony into the sect: First, a monstrous toad appeared to the Cathar novice. This was followed by the appearance of an ice-cold pale man. When the novice kissed the pale man, all traces of the Christian faith would depart from his heart. After a banquet celebrating the reception of the new member, a black cat appeared. All those attending the initiation festivities offered it the anal kiss. Finally the lights were extinguished, signaling the beginning of an orgy that included homosexual congress. The intensity of Gregory's accusations was matched only by the apparent sincerity of his belief in the charges—and the suffering that awaited those against whom such charges were leveled.

FIG. 8.3. Mural of the Last Judgment from the Cathedral of Albi (Vere Chappell). This detail shows the Earth realm under the sway of the demonic powers of the evil Manichaean creator god. On the other hand, it also accurately reflects the horrors suffered by the Cathars at the hands of their fellow Christians during the thirteenth century.

FIG. 8.4. Ladder to Heaven (12th century). This is a medieval illustration to a sixth century Byzantine monastic text. Byzantine doctrines formed the basis of the Bogomil heresy that later influenced the dualist Cathars. The souls of the wicked are shown being dragged down to the pit of Hell by black devils, while the good and the faithful continue their ascent to Heaven.

Fig. 8.5. Foix Castle (Vere Chappell). A Cathar fortress in Southern France.

Medieval European dualists were certainly not Manichaeans in the sense of an unbroken tradition dating back to 242 when the Persian mystic Mani proclaimed himself messiah. Mani divided the world into good and evil, darkness and light. He identified the earth as the kingdom of darkness under the reign of Satan. The only hope for man lay in intense ascetic practices by which he could remove the shackles of the dark force and arise to the kingdom of light. After thirty years of preaching, Mani was crucified and his body stuffed with straw on the recommendation of Magian religious leaders.

In reality, the eleventh-century heresies were isolated and independent of each other. While they shared certain features in common—most notably dualism, anticlericalism, asceticism, antimaterialism, idealism, iconoclasm, and revulsion at ecclesiastic corruption—there was no united ideology such as would later emerge among the Cathars.

The first record of the Cathars comes from Germany in the mid–twelfth century. "[T]he heresy was an ideology, with a body of belief and practice, potentially supra-national, impersonal, exceeding in durability the individual, idiosyncratic teachings of this or that charismatic personality, which had hitherto formed the stuff of the heretical episodes recorded by Western chroniclers."[2]

The Cathars were mystical Christians who believed in the direct, personal experience of God as the basis of all spiritual progress. Their origins trace back to the tenth-century Bulgarian dualist Bogomils, who disputed with the Byzantine Church. Both groups had much in common with the Christian Manichaeans of the fourth century. Most Cathars were moderate dualists—in other words, they believed that God was stronger than Satan, that God had allowed Satan to create the world, and in the end would crush all works of evil. On the other hand, it is easy to see how a

FIG. 8.6. OPPOSITE:
Albi Cathedral interior
(Vere Chappell).

FIG. 8.7. The jaws of Hell
(13th century). This horrifying
image of the damnation of the
wicked in Hell presents another
sobering and terrifying look
into the internal dynamics of
the medieval religious psyche.

radical dualist—one who perceived evil as an exactly coequal force—could tend toward the type of Satanic worship of which many moderate dualists were falsely accused.

Cathars taught that Satan or Lucifer created mankind from clay, and that the God of the Old Testament was in fact Satan. They therefore rejected the Old Testament. They believed the human soul was a fallen angel trapped in a material body, while the true spiritual body remained in Heaven. Through gnosis, or knowledge, the

soul could be united with spirit. Without gnosis, the soul would be condemned to migrate to another body in an endless succession of agonizing rounds of material imprisonment.

Cathars believed that matter was intrinsically evil and incapable of redemption. The first woman was tempted to commit the sexual act and thereby the soul was lost; sexual intercourse was the greatest sin because it perpetuated material evil. They rejected all belief in Hell or Purgatory; imprisonment within a physical body was punishment enough. They viewed Jesus as an emanation, or an angel, sent by God out of pity for fallen humanity to teach man the means of escape. Jesus was a part of God—neither God Himself nor man. His body was a projected illusion; pure spirit would have no contact with impure matter. Christ neither suffered nor died on the cross. The cross was an evil symbol of materiality to be despised, not venerated. The concept of Christ's physical resurrection was rejected. The Roman Church was built on the false worship of the creator God, in fact, of Satan. The Mass was rejected as a ritualized worship of matter.

The Cathar elect, the "Perfect," followed the true message of Christ—to reduce one's contact with the material world. They rejected the Church with all its hierarchy. Cathar initiates wandered throughout southern France as simple ascetics. They embraced a strict vegetarian diet, intensive fasting, and a life of poverty. Women had full clerical equality, although the diocesan hierarchy was all male. The oath of the Perfect, known as the *consolamentum*—the baptism of fire or of the spirit, the superior baptism promised in the New Testament—was ritually administered. A copy of the New Testament was placed on the candidate's head so that its message could infuse the psyche, while the initiator recited invocations and adorations of the Holy Spirit, directly transmitted to the candidate through the laying on of hands. The "kiss of peace" was exchanged among the Perfect administering the ritual and any simple Cathar believers present.[3]

The Catholic baptism of water mimicked the lower baptism of John the Baptist, who himself stated it was inferior to the baptism of fire: "I indeed baptize you with water unto repentance: but he that cometh after me is mightier than I, whose shoes I am not worthy to bear: he shall baptize you with the Holy Ghost, and with fire."[4]

The fact that Catholic baptism was performed on an infant without free choice rendered it meaningless. Worse, it was a link to Satan through the corrupt church. Cathar teachings were based solely on their interpretation of the New Testament. They traced their lineage to the Eastern churches mentioned in the Acts of the Apostles and in the Apocalypse.

The Perfect participated in a monthly rite of collective confession, known as the *apparellamentum*, before Cathar deacons or bishops who traveled throughout Cathar territories to administer this sacrament. The spiritual renewal and purification offered to the Perfect by the ceremony also provided the opportunity for the Cathar hierarchy to collect information on the state of various territories. The Cathar episcopate was responsible for the formal training of the Perfect in missionary and liturgical work.

The Perfect, or "Good Men," were materially sustained by the rank-and-file Cathar believers, those who hesitated to embrace the rigorous lifestyle to which the Perfect were bound. The Perfect were held in the highest esteem by Cathar believers, much as are Catholic saints. The *medioramentum* was an act of ritual adoration of the Perfect made by believers. Under the Cathar doctrine, those unwilling to undertake the oath of the Perfect were in the thrall of Satan. Prayers were therefore ineffective unless rendered by the Perfect.

Many Cathars took the *consolamentum* on their deathbeds, thus avoiding the danger of breaking their vows. In the final years of the fourteenth century when Catharism was all but wiped out, the practice of *endura* became increasingly common. This involved suicide by starvation by

FIG. 8.8. Albi Cathedral (Vere Chappell). The city of Albi was the center of the Languedoc and the initial target of the Albigensian Crusade.

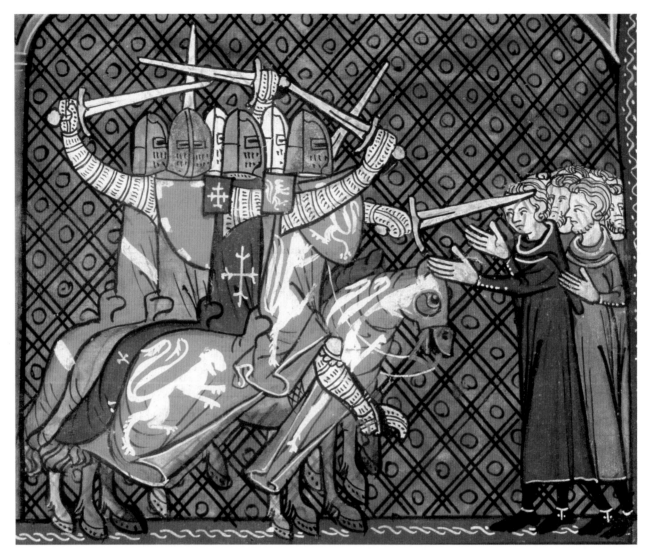

FIG. 8.9. The Albigensian Crusade (14th century). It is instructive to compare this image with all the other battle scenes in this book. Here it is an unarmed group that is attacked by the warriors.

one who had just taken the *consolamentum* and who was determined not to prolong the possibility of failure to live up to its rigorous demands nor to be captured and forced to renounce by the authorities.

Prior to the persecutions, the sect spread easily through Germany, southern France, and northern Italy. The Muslim presence in the Languedoc in the first half of the eighth century may have had something to do with the region's traditional religious tolerance and relaxed sexual mores. The simple and pious Cathars were perceived by their neighbors as motivated by spiritual concerns alone—no tithing, demands for material possessions, or political power accompanied their gentle faith. No churches were required. The apparent ethical superiority of the Cathar movement presented a very real threat to the Church. Cathar support has been estimated at ten to twelve percent of the population of Albi.[5] A number of noble families of the Languedoc were Cathar allies, further encouraging the growth of the sect among their dependents, either by active endorsement of Cathar preaching efforts or passive acquiescence in the spread of the heresy.

Certain aspects of Cathar belief worked against the growth of the sect. They rejected marriage as perpetuating the reign of Satan. So violent were their feelings that they sometimes mocked pregnant women as carrying demons in their bellies and declared women who died pregnant incapable of salvation. They rejected the eating of food produced by sexual means, although they ate fish, which they believed reproduced asexually. The Perfect were enjoined to strict celibacy. The antisexual, antifamily teachings of the Cathars eventually contributed to their decline, as they were unable to replenish their membership by the most natural means available. Another article of faith that worked against their growth was their uncompromising rejection of materialism. Cathar belief offered scant comfort

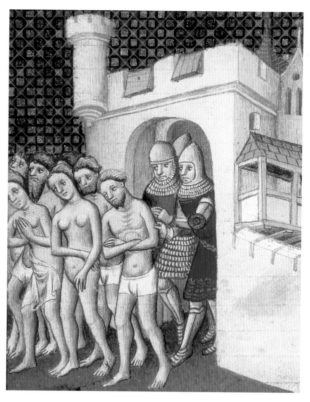

Fig. 8.10. The expulsion of the Albigensians from Carcassone (15th century).
Fig. 8.11. BELOW: Carcassone today (Vere Chappell).

FIG. 8.12. The famed castle of Montségur (Vere Chappell). One begins to get a sense of the independent power base represented by the Cathar movement. This should be factored in with any attempt to understand the root motivations of the Crusade.

to the poor, who were not attracted to a movement that remained unconcerned with bettering either their poverty or social status. Finally, a tinge of hypocrisy colored Cathar behavior during the persecutions. The strict oaths against the shedding of blood by the Perfect forced them to rely on the theoretically less pure Cathar faithful for defense against the military assaults of their enemies.

The efforts of the Church to counter the heretics had grown increasingly well organized since the preaching campaign in the Languedoc by Bernard in 1145 (he also suspected Cathars of libertinage) and the sporadic burnings by local bishops, priests, and even vigilantes among the townsfolk terrorized by the threat of demonic alliance. In 1206, two Castilian clergymen, Bishop Diego of Osma and his subprior, the canon Dominic de Guzman, volunteered to undertake a preaching campaign modeled on vows of poverty and simplicity like the campaigns of the first- and second-century apostles. They argued and debated with the heretics and traveled widely throughout the land. In 1207, Diego returned to Spain, while Dominic continued with his efforts. He later became the founder of the Dominican Order.

In 1208, the murder of a papal legate by an officer of the pro-Cathar nobleman Count Raymond VI of Toulouse so angered Innocent that he demanded a crusade against the Cathars, offering indulgences to those who committed to at least forty days of military service. This crusade was an attractive proposition when compared to the rigors demanded by military service in the Holy Land. Travel was effortless. Forty days was an extremely modest commitment for the remission of sins. Killing defenseless heretics seemed far less dangerous than fighting Arab warriors. Finally, the pope suggested that the property of landowners who supported and protected the heretics

might be seized, and the Languedoc was known to be filled with appreciable wealth.

Southern France was particularly susceptible to the political tensions caused by the declining power of feudal nobles and the corresponding increase in the power of the Capetian king, complicated by the ambitions of the indigenous clergy and the pope. The northern invasion of the Languedoc broke the power of the local southern nobility and paved the way for the extension of Capetian rule over this heretofore independent region.

Following the culmination of two decades of active military aggression, the Inquisition was officially born in the year 1233. "It cannot be repeated too often that the Albigensian Crusades did not wipe out heresy. They killed some of the 'perfect'; they ruined many of the protectors of the Cathars and so they prepared the way for the really effective attack on heresy—the Inquisition."[6] Gregory IX assigned the task of pursuing heresy to the Dominicans, granting them full power to make judgments, assigning them to work in specific dioceses of southern France, and appointing a special papal legate responsible for heresy to assist in their efforts.

Death was considered the proper remedy for heretics in order to root out the powers of the devil and his demonic spawn, and thereby protect the larger Christian community from the spiritual treason of the minority. Accusations of heresy rapidly became a convenient and effective smear against enemies. The flames of the Inquisition and the sword of intolerance would rage against the Cathars for over one hundred years. The last Cathar community of Perfect at the mountain stronghold of Montségur fell to renewed military campaigns in 1244. By 1325, Catharism seems to have been completely stamped out as a recognizable religious form.[7]

FIG. 8.13. View from Puilarens Castle (Vere Chappell). The beauty, vastness, independence, and wealth of this region would present a tempting target to the papal and monarchical consolidation underway during the thirteenth century.

Participation in the Albigensian Crusades was one of the most shameful activities of the Templars. It proved to be a dress rehearsal for their own destruction. Though rationalization may make nearly anything palatable, the Templars lent their efforts to the wholesale extermination of Christians. Although they acted at the behest of Innocent III, their actions thoroughly violated the very principles upon which their Order was founded. This medieval anticult pogrom was the occasion for the legendary reply of the papal legate, Arnaud Amaury, to soldiers concerned about distinguishing between Cathars and Catholics, "Kill them all, God will know his own." Although the literal occurrence of this statement has been disputed, the learned Amaury may actually have been quoting from two biblical verses: the first a letter from Paul to Timothy, "The Lord knoweth them that are his," in which Paul makes reference to a statement by Moses on the eve of battle, "Even tomorrow the Lord will shew who are his, and who is holy; and will cause him to come nearer unto him; even him whom he hath chosen will he cause to come near unto him."[8]

CHAPTER 9

✠

The Fifth Crusade and Saint Francis

Innocent was followed by Pope Honorius III, who continued to shower the Templars with his support for the next eleven years. Events in the Holy Land left numerous opportunities for diplomatic maneuvers by the Order to consolidate its power and forge alliances to help rebuild itself. Templars looked after their own interests and developed their remaining holdings into self-sufficient feudal communities. Castles were reinforced in keeping with the lessons of siege. The skill with which Saladin's sappers had been able to undermine castle walls was not forgotten. Castle Pilgrim at Atlit, between Jaffa and Haifa, marked the ultimate in medieval castle design. Construction began under the Templar Grand Master William of Chartres in 1217. Built on a promontory, the castle was surrounded on three sides by the sea and could hold out indefinitely against land-bound armies. It was never taken by an enemy and is today the site of an Israeli naval base.

FIG. 9.1. Castle Pilgrim at Atlit.

FIG. 9.2. Francis of Assisi at the court of the Ayyubid sultan al-Kamil (15th century). St. Francis attempted to convert the sultan, the brother of Saladin, to the Christian faith. The sultan sought Francis's help in lifting the siege at Damietta.

Fig. 9.3. Matthew Paris illustrates the battle at Damietta (13th century).

The Fifth Crusade began in 1217. It was a chaotic multinational task force composed of volunteers from Cyprus, Hungary, Italy, France, England, Holland, and Austria. The Crusaders attempted to take the Egyptian city of Damietta, hoping that a strategic victory against the Ayyubid sultan al-Kamil would allow them to successfully continue on to Jerusalem. The overall commander of this crusade was a papal legate, a Spanish cardinal named Pelagius. His inept handling of tactical matters allowed the Christians to virtually snatch defeat from the jaws of victory. The underlying assumption defining the strategy pursued by Pelagius and Pope Honorius was the late Pope Innocent's interpretation of Muhammad as the Great Beast prophesied in Revelation, whose evil empire would fall of its own accord. Thus the counsel of the Templars, the Hospi-

tallers, and any other qualified military leaders could be ignored in favor of religious prejudice.

Francis of Assisi visited al-Kamil at Cairo during the siege of Damietta. Through Francis, the sultan offered the Christians a truce. If they would leave Egypt, he would return the True Cross (taken by Saladin at Hattin) and give them the area around Galilee and the whole of central Palestine, including Jerusalem. Pelagius refused, believing it was sinful to negotiate with the infidel. The more sophisticated military leaders knew that Jerusalem would be in a strategically indefensible position because the sultan insisted on keeping two castles that could be used for future Islamic attacks. They also reasoned that the sultan must be weaker than they had estimated if he was willing to offer such favorable terms. They attacked Damietta with renewed enthusiasm and

FIG. 9.4. Medieval siege (14th century). The army shown here is using a weapon known as a "counterweight trebuchet" to fling heavy rocks at castle walls in an effort to open breaches in its defenses. The device is depicted smaller than it would be if the proportions of the illustration were more accurate. The Templars used such a machine during the attack at Damietta.

the city fell in November 1219, upon which they learned that it had been ravaged by plague.

Templar Grand Master William of Chartres had died that summer of complications from wounds. He was succeeded by Pedro de Montaigu, whose leadership inspired morale and confidence among the Templars. However, Pelagius insisted on holding the army within a twenty-mile radius of Damietta for the next two years, to the increasing disgust of the military leaders. Since the Templars were bound by their strict allegiance to the pope, they were forbidden to disobey his direct representative no matter how incompetent he might have been.

Finally, motivated perhaps by the anger and impatience of his allied forces, Pelagius ordered the assault force of over six hundred ships and

nearly fifty thousand troops to move against Cairo in July 1221. He could not have chosen a worse moment, as the annual inundation of the Nile was due. After a twelve-day march, the Frankish armies came to a plain from which vantage point they were able to see the Muslim army that had surrounded them undetected throughout their march. The Crusaders attempted to retreat only to have the Muslims open the Nile flood gates, nearly wiping them out. The Fifth Crusade ended in complete disaster. While al-Kamil generously offered to return the True Cross as part of the truce ending the Crusade, it was apparently of so little value to Islam that it had been misplaced over the decades. The Sultan ordered a careful search but it was never recovered.[1]

CHAPTER 10

✝

The Sixth Crusade and Frederick II

The Sixth Crusade was led by Frederick II in 1228. Frederick was an intriguing and exotic personality who spoke six languages fluently, including Arabic. He was liked and respected by the Muslims. He enjoyed long-standing friendships with various members of Islamic royalty, kept a harem in Sicily, and was schooled in Arabic philosophy and mathematics. He had little interest in Christianity, although as a child he had been the pupil of Cencio Savelli (later Pope Honorius III), who maintained a lifelong affection for Frederick despite their differences. Frederick was known to his contemporaries as *Stupor Mundi,* the "Marvel of the World." Crowned king of Germany by Innocent III in 1215, he immediately announced his intention to go on a crusade. This commitment seems to have been part of a strategy to retain papal favor while consolidating his rule in the Lombard region. In 1220, he was crowned Holy Roman Emperor by Pope Honorius III without yet having troubled himself with crusading. In 1225, he was married to the daughter and heiress of John of Brienne, king of Jerusalem. John apparently assumed the marriage would encourage Frederick finally to begin his crusade. Still he delayed.

In 1227, Honorius died. He was succeeded by Gregory IX, who immediately ordered Frederick to fulfill his promise to begin the crusade. When Frederick quickly returned, claiming illness, Gregory did not believe him. He excommunicated Frederick both for his premature return and his military efforts against the Templars and other loyal Catholics in the short time he was away.

Frederick set off again in June 1228, this time presenting the slightly absurd picture of an excommunicated king leading a crusade while the pope

FIG. 10.1. Frederick II (13th century).

sent an army against him in Sicily. Frederick's resolve to fight a crusade for two years was initially received with enthusiasm by the Templars and Hospitallers. Yet soon after his arrival in Acre, a letter from the pope ordered the Templars to play no part in Frederick's effort because of his excommunication. The pope soon sent another letter to the Templars announcing that he had just excommunicated Frederick a second time. It was forbidden for an excommunicate to take part in a crusade.

Although the Templars were bound by their vows of obedience to follow the pope's orders, they understood that any changes Frederick might effect in the balance of power with the Muslims would carry great consequences. Therefore they felt they needed full knowledge of his moves, and in the event of any military or territorial gains, they wanted to be included. Thus they decided on a compromise: they rode one day's journey *behind* Frederick so they could not be accused of marching *with* him. Later they marched alongside him. The terms of this arrangement were that Frederick would stipulate that his orders were being given in the name of God, rather than in his own name, that of an excommunicated emperor!

In February 1229, Frederick negotiated a ten-year treaty with al-Kamil for the return of Jerusalem and a corridor of land leading to the Mediterranean. In addition, the sultan agreed to the return of Nazareth, western Galilee, and the lands around Sidon and Bethlehem. In March 1229, Frederick crowned himself king of Jerusalem. The very next day, the archbishop of Caesarea excommunicated the entire city of Jerusalem for harboring the excommunicate emperor.

Although Frederick negotiated his treaty in the name of all Franks, he never received their permission to do so. The Templars were angry that the site of their original Temple would remain in Muslim hands. The treaty also forbade the military orders from making improvements on a number of their most important castles. The holy war against the infidel was the raison d'être of the military orders, and Frederick had just undermined it. Feelings were so strained between him and the Templars that he feared for his life and left Jerusalem after only a two-day stay.

Jerusalem had been placed in a strategically unsound position by Frederick's treaty, particularly for those less able than he to exercise diplomatic finesse with the Muslims. The Templars joined in a plan with the Patriarch of Jerusalem to take back Jerusalem in the name of the pope. Although they quickly reconsidered and withdrew from the plan, Frederick learned of their activities. He called them traitors, expelled them from Acre, and disarmed them to the extent that he was able. He helped strengthen the strategic position of the newly arrived Teutonic Knights, a German military order founded in 1198, and patterned after the Templars.

The pope, meanwhile, had undertaken a crusade against Frederick in Italy. The Templars attempted to persuade Sultan al-Kamil to turn against Frederick. Furious, Frederick attacked Acre and attempted to take Castle Pilgrim at Atlit, which survived his assault because of the superiority of its design. Finally, on May 1, 1229, the pressures to protect his kingdom from the pope forced Frederick to return to Europe. He continued his campaign against the military orders in Sicily, confiscated property belonging to the Templars and Hospitallers, and managed to regain the territory that had been lost in his absence.

The situation of the Templars improved in Outremer during the decade that Frederick's truce was in effect. The Order received further grants

FIG. 10.2. Acre. One of the most important and hotly contested strategic locations throughout the entire period of the Crusades.

of castles and lands. The success of their European wealth-building and recruitment efforts allowed them to undertake the defense and management of Latin interests in Syria. They began to involve themselves again in the shipping and protection of pilgrims and merchandise traveling from Europe. Skirmishes with the Muslims replaced major campaigns. The truce ended in 1239, and the Muslims retook Jerusalem, exactly as the Templars had predicted.

While the various treaties of the post-Hattin period had been of considerable help in rebuilding European strength, internal divisiveness among the Franks seemed to be working equally hard to undermine it. Widespread charges of abuse of power were made against the Templars. They were accused of contributing to the loss of cities and castles and weakening commerce because of their feuding with other military orders and the Italian merchant corporations. Violent confrontations between the military orders sparked by rivalry and jealously frequently erupted in bloodshed. In 1230, the Assassins assisted the Hospitallers in their military efforts against Bohemond IV. His successor, Bohemond V, wrote to Pope Gregory IX complaining of the alliance between the Hospitallers and Assassins. Gregory sent letters to the archbishop of Tyre and the bishops of Sidon and Beirut demanding that both the Templars and Hospitallers cease any alliances with the Assassins.

In 1240, the Templars successfully negotiated with the Ayyubid sultan of Damascus for possession of the castle of Safed in Galilee in return for an alliance with him against his rival, the Ayyubid sultan of Cairo. Safed was a powerful strategic prize, and the Hospitallers were jealous of the Templar gain. Allied with Richard of Cornwall, brother-in-law of Frederick II, the Hospitallers negotiated a treaty with the sultan of Cairo that, although it included the return of Jerusalem, was otherwise hostile to Templar interests. Later that year in Acre, fighting broke out between the Templars and Teutonic Knights and grew so violent that the Templars burned a church belonging to the Teutonic Knights. In 1242, a virtual civil war between Templars and Hospitallers led to battles in the streets between rival order members

throughout Outremer. The Templars laid formal siege to the Hospitaller compound at Acre.

Juxtaposed with conflicts between the military orders were conflicts between the various political powers. The interests of the pope and the allied Capetian dynasty were often in overt conflict with those of the Hohenstaufen dynasty under Frederick. The Palestinian baronage represented another source of disharmony. The barons had been established for a century and a half, and from their point of view, their political priorities were mature. Finally, the merchants of Venice, Genoa, Pisa, and Barcelona were engaged in corporate rivalry with each other, and they frequently aligned themselves severally with rival political or military interests.

The Ayyubid dynasty itself was in a virtual civil war between Cairo and Damascus, with

FIG. 10.3. Departure of the Templars (12th century). The knights bearing Templar insignia are shown heading off to battle in Syria in this fresco from the Templar chapel in Cressac, France.

FIG. 10.4. A battle scene showing Christian fighting Christian (19th century).
Dissensions and war between rival crusading factions would become an
increasingly severe problem throughout the thirteenth century.

FIG. 10.5. Prisoner march (13th century). Matthew Paris illustrates the defeat at Gaza in 1239 when the Templars and Hospitallers were blamed for not giving more assistance to French crusaders. Both military orders had advised against the expedition. Here the defeated Franks are led off as Muslim prisoners for later ransom or enslavement.

smaller sultanates variously allied with the larger combatants. Alliances were frequently proposed to the Franks by the conflicting Muslim powers. This had the net result of further exacerbating conflicts among the already disunited Christians. Gregory IX was attempting to gain support in Europe for a new crusade. A few nobles, such as Count Theobald of Champagne, responded to his call and made exploratory journeys to the Holy Land. These potential Crusaders walked into a situation so complex that it eliminated any preconceptions they may have entertained about a simple conflict between Christian and infidel.

Then the Khwarazmian Turks made their appearance in the area. This warrior tribe originally came from the isolated region of Khwarazm, some five hundred miles northeast of Alamut in the upper Oxus River (mod. Amu

Darya) area south of the Aral Sea. They had waged a campaign against the Assassins in Persia in 1198. The great Mongol leader Genghis Khan had been extending his empire westward by the fearsome power of the Mongol sword. In 1221, the Khan's armies had succeeded in driving the Khwarazmian Turks into exile, turning them into a roving mercenary band. In 1244, they were hired by the sultan of Cairo to storm Jerusalem, which they conquered in July. Only three hundred residents escaped the slaughter and pillage. So terrible was the Khwarazmian threat that the Templars and Hospitallers laid aside their differences. They cooperated with the baronage to raise a united Frankish force, which was joined by the army of the sultan of Damascus.

On October 17, 1244, the Khwarazmian Turks and the armies of the sultan of Cairo faced

FIG. 10.6. The victory of the Khwarazmian Turks at La Forbie in 1244 (13th century). This was an epic battle in which the Khwarazmians were allied with the armies of the Ayyubid dynasty of Cairo. A rare unity prevailed among the European military orders and the Palestinian baronage, and these forces were allied with the armies of the Abbassid dynasty of Damascus. The loss at La Forbie was one of the more memorable defeats of the Western forces during the two hundred years of the Crusades. The Templar bearing the Piebald Standard (at right) is shown fleeing the field in the face of the overwhelming force of the enemy.

the assembled Templars, Hospitallers, Palestinian baronage, and the armies of the sultan of Damascus at La Forbie near Gaza. The combined Christian and Damascene army suffered terrible losses. Grand Master Armand de Peragors was blinded and taken prisoner. The post-Hattin Christian gains of the last half century were virtually wiped out. Back in Europe, Frederick II blamed the Templars for not supporting his alliance with the Egyptians. He accused them of treason for their support of the Damascenes, angrily stating (apparently quite disingenuously in view of his own extensive Muslim friendships) that the Templars entertained Muslim princes with great pomp and allowed Muslim visitors to perform their unholy invocations of Muhammad within the gates of the Temple.

FIG. 11.1. The Battle of Mansourah (Detail, 15th century). The Crusaders were introduced to Baybars at Mansourah. This Mameluke general would later be responsible for their final defeat.

CHAPTER 11

✠

The Seventh Crusade and Baybars

The last great crusading effort began under the French king Louis IX after the defeat at La Forbie. Louis, born in 1214 in southern France, was an intensely spiritual man who was canonized twenty-seven years after his death. He brought a holy passion for the Crusades that seemed to hearken back to the victorious First Crusade, well before the cynicism and disappointment engendered by defeat, diplomatic maneuvering, and the enormous financial drain had taken their toll. Louis's enthusiasm, sincerity, and piety allowed him to overcome the contemporary attitude and gain support for a new effort. The Templars were instrumental in helping him finance the crusade and organize its logistics. Renaud de Vichiers, the Templar Preceptor of France, was a personal friend of the king. Louis set sail in August 1248, accompanied by de Vichiers, and arrived in Cyprus in September.

There they were joined by Grand Master Guillaume de Sonnac and a group of knights who had sailed from Acre. An

FIG. 11.2. Louis IX sets off for the Crusade.

emir representing the Egyptian sultan contacted Guillaume in an attempt to negotiate a peace treaty. When Louis learned of this, he forbade the Templars from continuing the discussion. Like Pelagius before him, Louis felt it was beneath Christian dignity to negotiate with the infidel. The plan of the Seventh Crusade mirrored that of the Fifth. It called for a landing at Damietta, with the intention of taking Cairo, then proceeding to Palestine.

Strong winds separated the attacking Christian fleet so that some galleys landed as far away as Acre. Louis, along with seven hundred knights, landed at Damietta on June 5, 1249. Fortunately for Louis, the illness of the sultan in Cairo, and the fierceness of the Crusaders' approach, frightened the Damiettians into abandoning their city to the small Christian force.

Also like Pelagius, Louis insisted on waiting in Damietta. He planned to let the Nile floods recede before proceeding to Cairo. Guillaume de Sonnac recommended instead that they attack Alexandria and then proceed to Cairo. The king overruled him. After months of waiting, the Christian army began the slow march to Cairo in late November. They were continually attacked by Muslim raiding parties along the way. Louis forbade any retaliation. Exasperated during one raid, Guillaume disobeyed the king and charged the Muslims. Six hundred enemy troops were killed, which heartened the Christians, and the march picked up tempo.

In December, the army reached the canal separating them from Mansourah, scene of the final defeat of the Fifth Crusade. On the other side of the canal were the armies of two leading Islamic generals, Fakhr ad-Din, a friend of Frederick II from twenty years earlier, and the Mameluke general Baybars. The Muslims held the Crusaders in place until February 1250, when part of the Christian force was able to ford the canal and attack the Muslim camp at dawn. Fakhr ad-Din was killed as he leapt naked from his bath. The Crusaders continued to Mansourah, where Baybars tricked them. His soldiers hid themselves within the walls of the town. The Christians

FIG. 11.3. Attack on Damietta (14th century). The army of Louis IX arriving at Damietta for the first battle of the Seventh Crusade.

unknowingly stormed through the gates, where they were ambushed, cut down nearly to the man. Of 290 Templar knights, only five survived. Count Robert of Artois, the fiery-tempered brother of the king, died along with three hundred secular knights. Meanwhile, the balance of the army crossed the river and were attacked by the Egyptian force. They suffered great casualties, including the loss of Guillaume de Sonnac, who was blinded and mortally wounded.

Louis hoped that the death of the Ayyubid sultan might plunge Egypt into revolt, but the

succession was peaceful. In April, Louis was forced to request negotiations for his army's survival. His offer was refused, and the Christians began their retreat. They were pursued by the Muslim army and lost thousands of men. Louis was captured and imprisoned. His courage and uprightness so impressed the Ayyubids that they agreed to release him on his promise that he would pay his ransom as soon as he was able.

However, on May 2, 1250, the new Ayyubid sultan, Turanshah, was murdered by his Mameluke bodyguards. The Mamelukes ("owned") were former white slaves, generally Turkish, European, and Russian. They had figured prominently in the Egyptian army since the twelfth century, participating in all of Saladin's campaigns. Now they were responsible for terminating his dynastic bloodline.

FIG. 11.4. King Louis IX arrives at Damietta (15th century). The massed Christian army, led by the French king in his resplendent armor, was about to face another humiliating defeat.

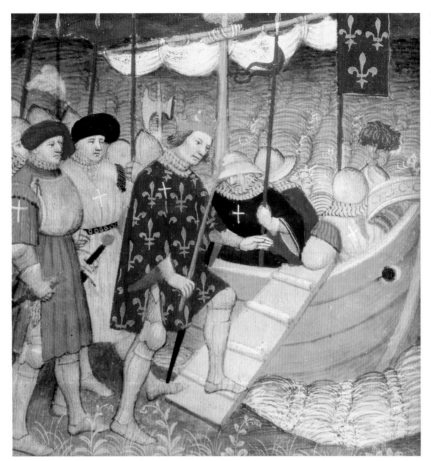

FIG. 11.5. Louis IX (15th century). The last great crusading monarch, Louis brought an inspired holy passion and sense of religious obligation to the Seventh Crusade that had been long lacking among the Christian forces.

The Mamelukes rushed to fortify their rulership of Egypt against a potential Christian rescue attempt of King Louis. The new Mameluke sultan Aybeg agreed to abide by the terms of the Ayyubid treaty to release Louis. The Franks surrendered Damietta, and Louis was released on May 6. One of his brothers was held for security while the king arranged his ransom payment.

Unable to raise the full amount required for the ransom, Louis's representatives approached the Templar Commander for a loan. He refused, saying that funds left in deposit with the Templars could only be returned to their rightful owners. However, Louis's friend Renaud de Vichiers, recently promoted to Marshal of the Temple, suggested that, under the circumstances, the French king might take the money by force, leaving the Templars no choice in the matter.

Louis's representative was rowed to the Order's flagship. He climbed aboard and threatened to smash open the Templar vault with an ax. De Vichiers immediately handed him the key to a strongbox in which were found the funds necessary for the payment.

De Vichiers became the new Grand Master. Louis made his headquarters at Atlit. The good relationship between the king and the military orders worked to Frankish advantage when an Assassin delegation arrived at Acre to demand a protection tribute from Louis. Three Ismailis holding daggers walked in front of a fourth bearing a shroud in a display calculated to frighten the king. The Assassins explained that other European heads of state who had dealings in the region, including the emperor of Germany and the king of Hungary, paid them tribute, as did the sultan at Cairo. They added that if Louis preferred not to pay, they would accept cancellation of their tributes to the Templars and Hospitallers.

Louis scheduled a second meeting to give himself time to consider the offer. At the second meeting, he was accompanied by the Grand Masters of the Temple and the Hospital, de Vichiers and William of Chateauneuf. Both Grand Masters were unrelenting with the Assassins and demanded a third meeting alone with them. The next day they warned the Assassin envoys that the king's honor had been insulted and that the Assassins were lucky not to have been tossed into the sea. The ambassadors returned to their leader. The Old Man replied by sending several gifts to Louis, the most important of which was the chief's own shirt. Since it was worn close to his body, it symbolized his intimacy with his new ally. He also sent a gold ring with his name engraved upon it. One gift, a set of beautiful crystal, was so heavily decorated with amber that it perfumed the room. Louis sent gifts in return, along with an Arabic-speaking friar named Yves the Breton who returned with the Assassin ambassadors to Masyaf. Here he was the guest of the Ismaili chief, probably Taj al-Din, with whom he discussed biblical and other religious matters. Yves later reported that his host was friendly, intelligent, and learned, and that he kept a Christian book by his bedside. Yves also explained the Syrian Ismaili doctrine that a favorable reincarnation would accrue to one who died in service to his lord.

Louis's wife gave birth to a son at Atlit in 1251. Renaud de Vichiers became the boy's godfather despite the prohibition against this in the Rule. In 1252, however, a conflict arose between Louis and the Templars that led Louis to publicly humiliate his friends. The warring Muslim sultanates of Cairo and Damascus had both sent delegations to enlist Frankish help against the other. Renaud presented Louis with a signed treaty the Templars had negotiated with their traditional Damascene allies that simply awaited the king's approval. Louis was furious at this perceived usurpation of his authority. While he was now sufficiently acclimatized to the realities of Outremer to accept treaties with the infidel, he leaned toward an alliance with Cairo. He hoped that he could thereby help to free the remaining members of his invading force still languishing in Muslim prisons. In anger, he forced the Templars to publicly assemble. He demanded they stand barefooted while de Vichiers loudly proclaimed to the Damascene ambassadors that he had made a treaty without the king's permission and therefore it was void. The Master and the Templars then knelt before the king, begged his forgiveness, and surrendered the Order's possessions to him. The Marshal of the Temple, who had done the actual negotiating, was banished from Outremer.

King Louis left the Holy Land in 1254. A disastrous civil war between Venetian and Genoese merchants erupted in the port city of Acre shortly thereafter. Acre had replaced Jerusalem as the headquarters of the military orders since the loss of that city to Saladin at the end of the twelfth century. During the course of the conflict, the Templars joined with the Teutonic Knights and the corporate powers of Venice and Pisa against the Hospitallers and the corporate powers of Genoa and Barcelona. This vicious internecine conflict, known as the Saint Sabas War, may have been responsible for the deaths of as many as twenty thousand Christians between 1256 and 1260.[1]

This period was also fraught with danger from the Mongol armies under the leadership of General Huelgu. The Mongols—descendants of the Huns who had attacked Rome eight hundred years earlier—began their conquest of Central

FIG. 11.6. Court of the Great Khan (14th century). The Khan and his family are depicted here in the *Jami al-Tawarikh* or *Universal History* by Rashid al-Din, the Muslim historian and biographer of Hasan-i-Sabah, founder of the Assassins.

FIG. 11.7. Mounted Mongol warrior. The fearsome Mongol armies were composed of courageous warriors trained since childhood in the arts of war.

Asia under Genghis Khan in the twelfth century. The great Mongol armies had first reached the Jaxartes River (modern Syr Darya) in 1218. In 1238, the Assassins sent envoys to France and England in a joint effort with ambassadors from the Abbasid caliph to enlist Christian rulers Louis IX and Henry III against the Mongols. Unfortunately for the Nizaris and Abbasids, the Euro-peans were at this moment seeking an alliance with the Mongols against them. By 1240, the Mongol assault had reached as far as western Iran and would soon progress to Georgia, Armenia, and northern Mesopotamia. In 1248, a Nizari Ismaili delegation to a Mongol assembly was turned away.

In 1252, Mangu, the grandson of Genghis

FIG. 11.8. The Mongol armies pillage Baghdad (14th century). This medieval version of "shock and awe" killed an estimated eight hundred thousand men, women, and children during forty days of looting.

Khan, was elevated as supreme Khan of the Mongols at Karakoram. He immediately ordered his younger brother Huelgu to set out against the Persian territories of the Assassins. In 1254, Mangu Khan received William of Rudrick, the Franciscan friar and ambassador of Louis IX. Louis wished to enlist Mongol support for the Christian armies of the Seventh Crusade. William learned that the great Khan was in fear for his life because he had heard that upward of forty Assassins in various disguises had been sent after him in retaliation for his campaign against them. Although Huelgu would not arrive in Iran until 1256, advance armies preceded him and battled their way through Nizari Ismaili territories.

The Mongolian army went on to attack the Abbasids at Baghdad in 1258. The Abbasid caliph al-Mustasim Billah surrendered and was slain after revealing the hiding place of the Abbasid fortune. The dynasty that had ruled Islam (at least in name) for half a millennium was crushed. The Mongolian army pillaged Baghdad for forty days, during which an estimated eight hundred thousand Muslims were massacred. In 1260, Huelgu seized the Ayyubid cities of Damascus and Aleppo. The devastation wrought throughout Islam by the Mongol slaughter is perceptible to this day.

The Mongols had also issued threats against the Templars and Hospitallers in 1255. The Templars, Hospitallers, and Teutonic Knights sent representatives to Europe to raise troops and funds. The Mongol ferocity caused anxiety throughout Europe. As events would later prove, however, the more dangerous threat was closer to home.

In 1259, the great Mangu Khan died. Upon learning of this, his brother Huelgu returned to Persia, leaving Ket-Buqa in charge of the Mongol army in Syria. The ruthless and extraordinary Baybars defeated Ket-Buqa in September of 1260 at Ain Jalut, just south of Nazareth. The hated Mongol army was at last driven from Syria. The Syrian Assassins, along with other Muslim forces, came to the aid of the Mamelukes in this decisive campaign. The Mameluke dynasty was established as the undisputed power in Syria as well as Egypt.

Baybars was born a Turkish slave. He rose to become a general in the Egyptian army. He murdered the Mameluke sultan Qutuz in 1260, soon after the victory at Ain Jalut, and seized the Egyptian throne. Baybars reigned until his death in 1277. He was a brave, ruthless, unscrupulous, and immensely talented military leader, responsible for some of the most important victories in the history of Islam. These included defeats of the Mongols, the Christians, and the Syrian Assassins.

In 1265, Baybars launched his offensive against Outremer. He took Caesarea, Haifa, and Arsuf. In 1266, he took Safed, which had grown during the last twenty-five years to a fiefdom that

FIG. 11.9. Baybars (Paul Kirchner). The great Mameluke sultan and general whose military prowess was unrivaled in the history of Islam.

included 160 villages and ten thousand peasants. "As soon as Baybars had taken control of the castle and the Templars, he gave them that night to decide whether they would choose conversion to the Islamic faith, or death. . . . [T]he Templars to a man chose death rather than give up the cross."[2] In 1268, Baybars took Beaufort, Antioch, Jaffa, Banyas, and Baghras, the first Templar castle in Palestine. In 1271, Chastel Blanc fell. By 1273, every Assassin fortress in Syria was also controlled by one of Baybars's lieutenants. The Mameluke dynasty ruled Egypt until their defeat by the Ottoman Turks in 1517.

CHAPTER 12

✠

The Eighth and Final Crusade

FIG. 12.1. King Edward I of England was a powerful monarch. His crusading experience would leave him an ardent supporter of the Templars.

Pope Clement IV pleaded in despair for help from all the European crowned heads. King Louis, now fifty-four years old and the father of eleven children, again answered the call of Christian duty. His family included his young grandson Philip, nicknamed le Bel, "the Fair," who had inherited his grandfather's good looks, if not his saintly character. Louis left France for his second crusade on July 1, 1270. He arrived at Carthage in Tunisia on July 17, where he contracted dysentery accompanied by fever and convulsions. On August 27 he died, whispering with his last breath, "Jerusalem, Jerusalem!"

Prince Edward of England led a crusading force that arrived in Acre on May 9, 1271. Baybars had just taken the Hospitaller fortress of Krak des Chevaliers and the Templar castle of Safita. When Louis and his army had arrived in North Africa the previous summer, Baybars was forced to turn his attention from his Palestinian campaign. Therefore the timing of Edward's entrance in the northern region seems to have contributed to Baybars's willingness to offer the Franks a ten-year truce. When the Templar Grand Master Guillaume de Beaujeu signed a nonaggression pact with Baybars, he effectively nullified the Templar role in Palestine.

Upon the death of Baybars in 1277, the Knights Templar were in a perilously weakened condition. The joint menace of Baybars and Huelgu had reduced the Franks to their lowest level of military

Fɪɢ. 12.2. Genghis Khan at battle (14th century). Rashid al-Din captures the ferocity of the great conqueror and founder of the dynasty that would wreak havoc in Muslim lands.

power in nearly two hundred years. Yet, perversely, the Order involved itself in a civil war in the county of Tripoli between 1277 and 1282. This unnecessary and wasteful abuse of power turned many in the Christian community irrevocably against Guillaume de Beaujeu and the Templars. Their distrust would have tragic consequences over the next decade, as we shall soon see.

In 1281, the Mongols launched a new attack against the Mamelukes. Baybars's successor, Sultan Qalawun al-Malik al-Mansur, offered the Franks a new ten-year truce in 1282 in an effort to avoid an alliance between the Franks and the Mongols. In violation of the truce, however,

Qalawun began to attack Frankish territories in 1285. By this time, the Christians of Outremer were reduced to a pathetic state in which all moral force had long since been spent. In place of the zeal to reclaim Palestine through Holy War in the name of Christ remained the desire for commerce with the Muslim infidel. In 1289, the residents of Tripoli invited Qalawun to intervene in their internal civil affairs. He humored them and made use of the opportunity to seize Tripoli. Guillaume de Beaujeu had been alerted to the sultan's intentions by his network of spies. He attempted to warn the Christians but had so discredited himself in their eyes that they refused to believe him. Qalawun destroyed the city and slew

FIG. 12.3. Muslim warriors (14th century). The Persian epic *Shahnama* by Firdawsi is an example of the existence and importance of the doctrines of chivalry in Islamic culture.

its inhabitants. Cynically, he declared that the truce was still in effect despite his own behavior. The weak and frightened Christians accepted this absurd statement.

In 1290, a riot broke out in Acre and several Muslims were killed. De Beaujeu was informed by his spy network that Qalawun was amassing an army to move against Acre. De Beaujeu proposed that Christian prisoners held by the military orders and the merchant powers be turned over to the sultan and blamed for the riots to placate the Mamelukes. Since the prisoners were already facing the death penalty, he reasoned this was an intelligent ruse to save the greater population. His plan, however, was rejected. De Beaujeu next privately negotiated with Qalawun to spare Acre for the price of one gold coin for each resident. When he announced this arrangement to the people, they pronounced him a traitor.

Qalawun died in November 1290 and was succeeded by his son, al-Ashraf, who swore to continue in his father's footsteps. On April 5, 1291, al-Ashraf laid siege to Acre. On April 15, Guillaume de Beaujeu led a night attack against the encamped Muslim army. The knights initially had the element of surprise in their favor, but in the darkness they became entangled in the Muslim tent ropes and were beaten back. On May 18, the Muslims broke through the city's defenses and entered the walls of Acre. The Templars fought valiantly against overwhelming force and de Beaujeu was mortally wounded.

Only the Templar castle at the southwest of the city remained in Christian hands. Surviving Templars assembled there along with some citizens of Acre who had joined them. The Marshal of the Temple, Peter de Sevrey, was in command. On May 25, al-Ashraf offered him and all occupants of the castle safe passage to Cyprus if they surrendered. De Sevrey agreed and opened the castle gates. The Mameluke soldiers went wild when inside, attacking men, women, and children indiscriminately. The Christians managed to fight them off. De Sevrey sent the Commander of the Temple, Theobald Gaudin, to Sidon with the remaining treasure and holy relics of the Order.

Al-Ashraf renewed his offer of safety. This time de Sevrey left the castle to discuss terms, only to be beheaded in sight of the remaining garrison. The sultan's troops stormed the castle, and on May 28, 1291, Acre fell. All present were killed.

FIG. 12.4. Muslim army attacks Acre (14th century). The battle at Acre in 1291 was the final defeat of the Western armies, effectively ending the medieval Crusades.

CHAPTER 13

✟

The Templars in Defeat

Theobald Gaudin was elected Master of the Order in Sidon. After a large Mameluke army appeared, he left for Cyprus carrying the Order's remaining assets. Sidon was abandoned on July 14. Tortosa was evacuated on August 3. On August 14, 1291, Castle Pilgrim was abandoned. The Holy Land was empty of Christian power for the first time in two hundred years.

Upon the death of Gaudin in April 1293, Jacques de Molay was elected the twenty-third and last Grand Master of the Knights Templar. Born in France in 1244, de Molay joined the Order in 1265 and was soon sent to the Holy Land. He was outspoken and critical of what he found there. He felt the business of the Templars was fighting the infidel and viewed any treaties with the Muslims as weakness at best, and treason at worst. He was openly disdainful of Guillaume de Beaujeu and his efforts at diplomacy. De Molay rigidly maintained his opinionated demeanor through the twenty-seven years of his service in the Order. He made a convincing appeal to the brethren of his own fitness to lead.

In 1294, de Molay left Cyprus for a three-year journey through Europe to meet with the heads of state of England, France, Naples, and Aragon, as well as the pope. He was working to gain support for the Order so that it could rebuild in preparation for a new crusade. He was successful in gaining some tax exemptions and import and export allowances from the various kings. Pope Boniface VIII mediated a dispute between the Templars and King Henry of Cyprus, who claimed authority over the Order because it was situated in his domain. The pope granted the Templars the same privileges on Cyprus they had held in

FIG. 13.1. OPPOSITE: Jacques de Molay (19th century). The final Grand Master of the Temple whose last years were wrapped in the many contradictions characteristic of the larger Templar story.

Syria. He urged King Henry to treat them well in consideration of their great suffering in defense of the Holy Land.

The Templars did their best to pursue their goals. A small garrison had been left at Ruad, an island two miles off the coast of Tortosa, in 1291. The Order worked to increase its naval capacity and took part in raids against the Muslims. The garrison at Ruad was gradually reinforced until 1302, when it was attacked and destroyed by a Mameluke naval force. As late as 1306, the Templars participated in a major political intrigue in Cyprus, aiding Amaury de Lusignan in deposing his brother, King Henry. The Hospitallers joined them on Amaury's behalf. The intention behind the participation of the military orders was to strengthen Cyprus as a crusading base against the Mamelukes. The Templars also supported efforts to build an alliance with the Mongols against the Mamelukes.

Long-held resentments against the Knights Templar were, however, now able to rise unchallenged to the surface. In defeat they became a convenient target. They had long been viewed with suspicion and distaste because of their unique papal privileges. In addition to isolating the Templars from the communities in which they lived, the Order's papal privileges tended to reduce the independence of local parishes. The papacy had extended its long tendrils directly into the lives of remote countryside towns and villages. The Templar privileges extended to both the noble-born knights as well as the lower-class serving brothers, some 90 percent of the Order's membership. The churlish behavior of which many of these men must have been guilty would have been another ready source of hostility from

FIG. 13.2. Return of a Crusader (19th century). Wearing the mantle of the Knights Templar, this mounted warrior personifies defeat.

FIG. 13.3. Maritime combat (13th century). Battle at sea between a Templar galley and a ship. The Hospitallers had a greater commitment to their naval fleet but the Templar navy was an important component of the Order's efforts.

their neighbors. Finally, the apparent extent of Templar wealth and power contrasted poorly with their overall record in battle.

The Templars were thoroughly identified with the Crusades. The obvious question of God's support for the Christian cause pressed more and more heavily on the pious heart as defeat was added to defeat. Disillusionment replaced enthusiasm and praise gave way to blame. As the success of the Crusades had been the cause of the incredible rise of the Templar star, so defeat would herald their tragic demise. They had suffered catastrophic losses in the past and recovered each time. But the loss of their assigned protectorate was a blow from which they never recovered. Bravery could not absolve defeat.

There was another problem. It is estimated the membership of the Order included some seven thousand knights, sergeants, serving brothers, and priests at this time. Associate members and allied individuals brought the number much higher. The Order possessed at least 870 castles, preceptories and houses.[1] Their independent, armed presence in Europe could not fail to produce tension. The Templars retained the power to declare war and make peace on their own terms.

They could not be ordered to fight for kings and were exempt from royal taxes and tolls. They stood apart as a feudal anachronism from the ever-growing central power of the monarchy.

PROPOSALS FOR UNIFICATION OF THE MILITARY ORDERS

The loss of Palestine acted as crisis often had before, becoming a catalyst for the drive for a new crusading effort. This time, however, it would carry sinister consequences for the Knights Templar. Europe had changed greatly during the period of the Crusades. Feudalism was evolving into nationalism, while Christianity was losing its iron grip on medieval culture. The considerable financial burden of the Crusades was finally encouraging monarchs and church leaders to seek relief. The leading powers came to the conclusion that a unification of the wealth and assets of the Templars, Hospitallers, and Teutonic Knights—including personnel and leadership—might combine to make a whole greater than the sum of its parts. King Louis IX had first advanced a proposal for unification of the military orders as early as 1248.

At the Council of Lyons in 1274, one of the

Fɪɢ. 13.4. Raymond Lull (14th century). This medieval theologian (ca. 1232–1315) was a fascinating figure. Known as "Dr. Illumatus," he was a member of the court of James I of Aragon until he became a hermit and later a Franciscan monk. Widely schooled in Muslim language and religion, he was also deeply versed in the Kabbalah and Alchemy. He has been considered by many occultists to have been a member of the Rosicrucian fraternity.

issues under consideration was a general overview of attitudes toward the Crusades. The guiding light of the council was the Spanish mystic Raymond Lull, a former knight who had became a preacher. Lull was also a Muslim scholar and linguist. He believed that Islam could be converted to Christianity, for the most part peaceably, by well-prepared preachers; however, he accepted that the process must involve a certain amount of force. He was a strong advocate of consolidating the military orders. Pope Gregory was apparently convinced by Lull's arguments, but Gregory died in 1276. Six short-lived popes followed over the next twelve years, so no further progress was made toward uniting the orders. In 1287, Lull first presented his ideas to the newly crowned French king, Philip IV.

PHILIP IV AND CLEMENT V

The grandson of King Louis IX, Philip the Fair, crowned in 1285 at the age of seventeen, had become the most powerful king in Europe. He was a man who understood power. He was

FIG. 13.5. King Philip IV, "Le Bel." The prime mover and arch enemy behind the destruction of the Order of the Temple.

manipulative, cunning, cold, intelligent, and determined, with an instinctive grasp of psychology and an almost modern appreciation for the power of the "Big Lie." At the same time that he embodied the psychological qualities of a ruthless politician, Philip was viewed as a semidivine being. The Church taught that the monarchy was appointed by God to rule the faithful; Philip had been anointed at his coronation with the legendary holy oil of the Capetian dynasty; he was known throughout Europe as "the most Christian King of France." These cultural beliefs appear to have been internalized within his own psyche.

Philip faced a very difficult financial situation. The ambitious growth of France as a world power had cost dearly. The lack of a predictable source of royal income was characteristic of the feudal economy. Philip exhausted himself with plans to overcome his chronic shortage of funds. His currency manipulations alone devalued the coin of the realm by two-thirds during the decade beginning in 1290. He inaugurated a plethora of new taxes including a national sales tax. He also levied special taxes on the Lombards and Jews, two wealthy minority groups from whom he was accustomed to borrow.

Philip's financial woes caused him to take the unprecedented step of levying taxes against the Church. This placed him in direct opposition to the equally ambitious Pope Boniface VIII. In 1296, Boniface issued a bull forbidding clerical taxation. Philip responded by prohibiting the export of bullion from France, thus effectively severing the flow of tithes to Rome. Boniface excommunicated Philip in 1303. The pope intended to place the entire nation of France under papal interdict. At this Philip balked. He brought legal proceedings against Boniface in France and sanctioned an armed arrest of the pope while Boniface vacationed at his summer residence in Anagni outside Rome. The raid, conducted with a force of sixteen hundred soldiers, occurred the day before the pope was to issue his bull against France. The frail eighty-six-year-old Boniface was imprisoned for three days before he was liberated by the populace of Anagni, but he died within a month of the attack.[2]

Guillaume de Nogaret had led the raid against Boniface. He had joined King Philip in the early 1290s. He was made "first lawyer of the realm" in 1302. De Nogaret was a fanatic who was expert in smearing his victims with accusations of magic, heresy, and sexual perversion—the appropriate contemporary shibboleths that could be used to incite the irrationality of the population.

Boniface was succeeded by Pope Benedict XI. In audience before Benedict, de Nogaret accepted full responsibility for the raid against Boniface. This allowed Benedict to lift Philip's excommunication but forced him to excommunicate de Nogaret. This presumably had little effect on the French lawyer because of the depth of his hatred for the papacy. Contemporary accounts stated that his parents were Cathars who had been burnt alive as heretics during the Albigensian Crusades.

Philip's extraordinary actions against the pope were dramatically illustrative of the struggle for power between secular kings and the papacy during the early fourteenth century. From the theocratic dreams of Gregory VII in 1073 to the impotence of Boniface in 1303, the battle had gradually been turning in favor of the monarchs.

Raymond Lull had modified his original emphasis on peaceful conversion of the infidel after the loss of Acre. In 1292, he advanced the idea of a new crusade to be fought by a unified military order commanded by Philip or one of his sons. The position of master of the new order

FIG. 13.6. Pope Boniface VIII. He was a casualty, or perhaps a martyr, in the medieval battle between Church and State.

was to be hereditary or appointive. The master would reign as king of Jerusalem. He would be known as Bellator Rex, the "Warrior King." Lull spent some years at Philip's court attempting to acquire support for his plan.

Pope Benedict XI died after only eight

CLEMENS V,
Burdegalensis, creat
Sedit an.8.mens.10.
Aprilis an.1314.Vac.

Bertrand? de Gotho,
die 5.Iunij an.1305.
dies 16. Obijt die 20
Sed.an.2.men.3.d.17.

FIG. 13.7. Clement V. This image seems to capture his weak and indecisiveness nature.

months in office. Philip succeeded in having the archbishop of Bordeaux, Bertrand de Got, elected as Pope Clement V in November 1305. Clement would become little more than a tool in Philip's ruthless hands. Of the twenty-four cardinals whom Clement would appoint during his papacy, twenty-three were French. By 1308, some three years after his accession, he had not yet visited Rome because of the incessant demands of the French king. Under pressure from Philip, Clement even moved his headquarters from Rome to Avignon in southern France. Avignon was owned by some of the pope's vassals. It served as the seat of the papacy through seven popes until 1377, a period known as the "Babylonian Captivity."

Philip's financial problems continued to mount. In June 1306, he announced that France would return to a full-valued currency, instantly tripling prices. Violent riots took place throughout Paris with angry mobs in deadly skirmishes with royal troops. Philip took refuge in the Paris Temple for three days, during which he was reminded firsthand of the military and financial strength of this kingdom within his own kingdom of France. (The previous year, Philip had sought membership in the Temple after the death of his wife. His application was refused, fueling his resentment against the Order.) His intractable financial problems drove him to another radical act that was to be a grim preview of coming attractions—Philip arrested every French Jew on July 21, 1306. This statewide operation, supervised by Guillaume de Nogaret, was successful in adding a great store of seized assets and wealth to the needy royal coffers, as well as canceling many debts the French king had owed to Jewish moneylenders.

Pope Clement V sent out letters on June 6, 1306, summoning the Grand Masters of the Templars and Hospitallers to an audience at Poitiers to discuss a new crusade. De Molay journeyed first to Paris, where he deposited his valuables at the Temple and met with the French king. Philip apparently flattered and deceived the old warrior, who left assured of the continued good relations between the Order and the French crown.

Jacques de Molay traveled on to Poitiers to meet the new pope. Philip had recently presented Clement with a series of terrible allegations of heresy and immorality against the Templars. Philip assured the pope these charges had been

FIG. 13.8. Avignon (Vere Chappell). Headquarters of the papacy from the reign of Clement V until 1377.

Fig. 13.9. Headquarters of the Templars in Paris (19th century).

made by a reliable witness, and he demanded that Clement hold a full papal inquiry into the matter. Clement informed de Molay of the situation. The Master was furious and incredulous, vehemently denying any wrongdoing. The pope was satisfied with his answers. De Molay returned to Paris for a secret chapter meeting in July 1307. A circular was sent throughout all Templar houses in France reminding the brethren of the Rule's prohibition against discussing any of the secrets of the Order. He again visited the pope at the end of August and may have aggravated the situation by demanding a full papal inquiry to clear the Order's name of the slander and suspicion under which he had been chafing.

CHAPTER 14

✠

Arrest and Trial

The primary original witness against the Templars was one Esquin de Floyran, a disaffected French Templar. Three other witnesses were found who supported his account, two ex-Templars and a cleric. Philip authorized twelve spies to join the Order in France during the summer of 1307, who allegedly reported back that the accusations against the Templars were true. A trickle of other witnesses came forward as well, each held in some form of disrepute by the Order.

Philip issued a sealed mandate on September 14, 1307 to his police officers throughout France. It called for discrete preparations to be made for the arrest of every French Templar at dawn on October 13, 1307. The warrant accused the Order of unspeakable crimes against God, Christ, the Church, Europe, and common decency through heresy, witchcraft, treason, and sexual perversion. The charges bore the characteristic hand of de Nogaret, whom Philip had promoted to chancellor of France and guardian of the king's seal. The intention of such a strongly worded document was to convince Philip's police to overcome their own scruples and act against these highly regarded men—their neighbors and friends.

To attach an air of legality to his actions, Philip claimed the arrest order had been prepared at the request of the Inquisitor-General of France, the Dominican friar Guillaume de Paris. While no direct evidence exists for this specific claim, Guillaume was an active participant in the affair. Philip had attempted to control the Inquisition in France for a decade, and Guillaume was his private confessor. Guillaume would have been within his legal rights as head of the Inquisition to seek the aid of the secular monarch to assist the Church in the matter of heresy.

On October 12, 1307, de Molay was honored as one of the pallbearers for the funeral of King Philip's sister-in-law. The next day, Friday the thirteenth, he and every Templar in France were in

FIG. 14.1. Arrest of the Templars (14th century). Swiftly and suddenly, the once-proud Templars were seized by the merciless talons of the French crown. Friday the Thirteenth henceforth became known as a day of bad fortune.

FIG. 14.2. The Church of Notre Dame (Vere Chappell).

jail. Of approximately five thousand French Templars, fewer than twenty escaped. Philip's precipitous arrests had the effect of avoiding a prolonged inquiry while the brethren were still at liberty and able to defend themselves by legal means. Philip next employed a sophisticated medieval version of "spin control." On the day after the arrest, Saturday, October 14, the masters of the university and cathedral canons were assembled in Notre Dame, where de Nogaret and others addressed them regarding the crimes for which the Templars had just been arrested. On Sunday, October 15, an invitation was extended to the French people to come to the garden of the royal palace, where they were addressed by spokesmen of the king and Dominican inquisitors. Similar town meetings were held throughout France to mold public opinion. On Monday, October 16, Philip sent letters to all kings and princes of Christendom to explain his actions and enlist their support against Templars in their own lands.

French "due process" at this time opened wide the gateway of judicial abuse. Torture was the legal and accepted method of conducting interrogations. The Inquisition exerted its brutality convinced of its divine mission. The Templars were doomed. The French secular officials who conducted the arrests were instructed to begin interrogation and torture at once. Within days, these tasks were transferred to the authority of the Inquisition. The monarchy participated to varying degrees depending on the regional personnel needs of the Inquisition.

The excruciating reality of medieval torture demands a descriptive paragraph. The technology of torture during this period included the rack, to which the ankles and wrists of the victim were tied with ropes attached to a windlass. As the crank was turned, the arms and legs would be progressively stretched until they dislocated from their sockets. Another infamous method of torture was the strappado. This involved tying the hands with a rope behind the back and throwing the other end of the rope over a ceiling beam. The victim would be hoisted upward and precipitously dropped—then yanked to a halt inches from the floor, cracking and dislocating arms, shoulders, wrists, and ribs. Weights might be attached to feet or testicles to increase the agony. Torture by fire was conducted by smearing fat on the soles of the feet and holding them to the flames. One unforgettable account of this procedure came from a Templar priest whose bones dropped out of his feet several days after the torture. He brought the bones to his hearing before the papal commission. Other forms of torture

FIG. 14.3. Torture (19th century). With no legal recourse, the Templars fell victim to the vindictive fury of the French king and the mania of the Inquisitors.

Fig. 14.4. Interrogation of de Molay (19th century). Can the modern reader perhaps forgive the vacillations and confusion of this tragic figure, victim of an almost childlike faith in the solicitude of the leader of his church and the laws of his nation?

involved such time-proven techniques as beating, starvation, diets of bread and water, sleep deprivation, restriction in irons or chains, unspeakable sanitary conditions, and verbal and psychological abuse. Many Templars died in prison—some took their own lives in desperation.

By October 25, two weeks of imprisonment had succeeded in preparing these fallen warriors for the first scene of the terrible tragedy that would crush them utterly over the next seven years. On that day, Grand Master Jacques de Molay admitted the Order's crimes to a prestigious assembly of legal scholars held at the University of Paris. While some believe de Molay confessed from fear of torture alone, in a letter

dated January 1308, he wrote that the brutality he had suffered included having the skin torn off his back, belly, and thighs.[1]

The next day, thirty more leaders and other handpicked Templars added their confessions to buttress de Molay's accounts. They testified that their ritual of reception included the denial of Christ, spitting on the cross, obscene kisses, and the worship of a hideous idol in the form of a human head. De Molay thanked the "Most Christian King Philip" for exposing these sins and wrote an open letter to the brethren, ordering them to confess.

On November 9, Hugh de Pairaud, Visitor of the Order, second-in-command to de Molay,

Fɪɢ. 14.5. Initiation of a Templar (19th century). An idealized depiction of the charges leveled against the Order. The Templars were perceived as the shadow-self of Europe.

FIG. 14.6. Baphomet (19th century). Éliphas Lévi stylized his occult Lord of Initiation after the legendary deity, variously described, said to have been secretly worshiped by the Templars.

confessed and mentioned the famous "Templar head" at length. He claimed to have carried it about from chapter to chapter in his journeys through France. He described it as having four feet, two in front and two in back. Others later claimed it was too terrifying to describe: that it had a beard; or a demon's face; or two faces with two beards; or three faces; that it was made of sil-ver with carbuncles in the eye sockets and a tex-ture of old skin; that it was completely smooth to the touch; that it was a painting or a small brass or gold statuette of the figure of a woman. The Templar head was stylized by Éliphas Lévi as the Devil Card of his Tarot—Baphomet, the andro-gyne Lord of Initiation.

Despite the thoroughness of the king's

FIG. 14.7. The Apotheosis of St. Ursula (15th century). Surrounded by the eleven thousand virgins of myth, Ursula begins her heavenly ascent.

search, only one head was turned up in the Paris Temple. This was a large, hollow, silver female bust, in which was found a skull, wrapped in a red linen shroud, with a label identifying it as "Caput LVIII" or "head no. 58." Testimony explained that it was the skull of one of the eleven thousand martyred virgins. This referred to the martyrdom of Saint Ursula, patron saint of virgins, and eleven of her companions during the early centuries of the Christian era. Due to a mistranslation of the text, eleven virgins became the eleven thousand of legend.[2]

Geoffroi de Gonneville, the fourth highest ranking dignitary of the Order, stated that the practice of denying Christ and defiling the cross was enjoined on the Order by the pledge of an evil Grand Master imprisoned by a Muslim sultan. To secure his release, the Grand Master swore to introduce the denial of Christ into the Order's reception ceremony henceforth. Later in the deposition, he opined that the custom may have been in imitation of Saint Peter's threefold denial of Christ.

One hundred thirty-eight depositions survive from the examinations held in Paris between October 18 and November 24, 1307. Of that number, only four Templars proclaimed their innocence. One hundred twenty-three Templars confessed to spitting on or near the cross. Yet the vast majority of French Templars were middle-aged members of the European support network, with no combat experience, who quickly confessed under torture or the threat of it and the demoralizing example of their leaders. At least twenty-five Parisian Templars died from torture during the fall of 1307.

Philip's appeal of October 16 to the other European monarchs to arrest the Templars was rebuffed. They did not believe him, being well aware of his character. Pope Clement's power was necessary to legitimize Philip's actions. The Church's imprimatur would allow Philip to rob

FIG. 14.8. Inquisition prison (19th century). The sense of darkness, despair, and utter hopelessness is rendered palpable by the artist.

FIG. 14.9. Auto da fé of St. Dominic (15th century). The founder of the Dominican Order presiding over the burning of heretics.

the Templars not only with impunity, but with sanctification. Clement appeared to take control of the proceedings. For their part, the Templars looked to the pope for protection from the persecution of the king and a fair hearing. De Molay clung to this misplaced hope for years.

Clement issued the bull *Pastoralis praeeminentiae* on November 22, 1307, which required the kings of England, Ireland, Castile, Aragon, Portugal, Italy, Germany, and Cyprus to arrest the Templars within their borders and sequester their property, *but* to do so in the name of the pope. Clement announced that he would investigate the charges against the Order, and that he would be especially pleased if they were proven baseless. The pope had placed himself in the center of the hurricane that Philip had unleashed. Philip undoubtedly hoped the matter might be over within a couple of weeks after the arrests. Clement's intervention stalled the proceedings for seven years.

The first papal investigations in France began with two cardinals sent by Clement in December 1307. The cardinals soon reported the shocking news that Jacques de Molay, Hugh de Pairaud, and sixty other brothers were retracting their earlier confessions made under torture.

By the terms of the Inquisition, the accused *were* guilty. There was little chance or interest in determining innocence. The accusation was the crime. There were no provisions for mounting a defense; no legal counsel was allowed. Witnesses were reluctant to testify on behalf of the accused lest they be branded as accomplices. Witnesses for the prosecution could remain anonymous. Confession was the only practical avenue—if no confession was received, torture would certainly follow. In rare cases where a confession was not obtained by torture, excommunication as a demonically inspired heretic would be followed

by burning at the stake. If a confession obtained by torture was retracted, the same punishment awaited the unfortunate soul, for he was perceived as a relapsed heretic and the revenge of Christ would follow. Confession and repentance allowed for a reconciliation with the Church prior to the imposition of punishment.

Clement suspended the French Inquisition in February 1308 to collect together the evidence and court records to date. He insisted that the proceedings against the Templars would be fairly conducted by an independent papal commission. King Philip insisted the Order was guilty. He and de Nogaret initiated a campaign of vilification and slander against the pope through anonymous pamphlets, accusing Clement of protecting heretics because of his own corruption. Philip convened the Estates General in May 1308. After a week of listening to de Nogaret's accusations, the two thousand representatives of the nobles, clergy, and commoners voted their support for Philip's actions and the destruction of the Order.

Philip traveled to Poitiers with a small armed force to discuss the matter with Clement and pressure him to capitulate. Clement responded that he would hold firm to his decision to handle the matter in a legal and proper fashion. He declared his hatred of heresy but spoke of his duty to fairness. Philip next tried conciliation. He would, of course, submit to Clement's authority, but since the pope had no jails, Philip would help by keeping the Templars in France's prisons. He arranged for seventy-two handpicked Templars to come before the pope and confess their crimes directly. This left Clement some latitude. He said that the confessions were convincing. Next, he split the inquiry into two separate categories.

Category one was a papal commission of inquiry to judge the Order as a whole, which would report to the Council of Vienne, scheduled to meet two years later. Category two involved reinstituting the Inquisition, suspended since February, to judge the guilt or innocence of individual Templars. This investigation would be conducted at the diocesan level by provincial councils presided over by the local bishop, who was appointed by the king. Thus Philip had control of the inquisitorial activities throughout France.

Despite Clement's various stratagems to save face and maintain the appearance of papal independence, he had little if any genuine concern for the members of the Order. On August 12, 1308, he released the articles of accusation against the Templars, *Faciens misericordiam*. The list included 127 offenses, many of which repeated others. The most serious charges were the following:

- That at the ceremony of reception (or sometime after the ceremony) the Order demanded its new members deny Christ, or Christ crucified, sometimes Jesus, God, the Virgin, or the Saints.

- That the Order taught that Jesus was not the true God, that he was a false prophet, that he had not suffered on the cross, that he had died not for the redemption of humanity but for his own sins, that neither the receptor nor the candidate could expect salvation through Jesus.

- That at the ceremony of reception, the candidate was told to spit on the cross, or an image of the cross or of Jesus. That they sometimes trampled the cross underfoot, or urinated upon it, both at the reception ceremony and at other times.

- That they adored a "certain cat" in contempt of Christ and the orthodox faith.

- That they did not believe in the sacraments of the Church.

- That Order priests did not properly consecrate the host nor speak the correct words during the Mass.

- That the Grand Master, or the Visitor, or even the Preceptors, claimed they could absolve members of sin.

- That there were a series of kisses during the ceremony of reception, by the candidate or by the receptor, either on the other's mouth, navel, bare stomach, buttocks, base of the spine, or penis.

- That homosexual relations were enjoined upon them as licit and that members were instructed that it was proper to submit to advances from brothers.

- That they worshiped and adored an idol as their God and savior. It was variously described as a human head, or heads, sometimes with three faces, or a human skull. It was believed the idol protected the Order, gave it riches, and caused the trees to flower and the land to germinate.

- That in their receptions, they surrounded the idol with a small cord that they then wore at all times around their waists, next to the shirt or on the flesh, in veneration of the idol.

- That the leaders of the Order punished anyone who refused to engage in improper behavior or who complained about the Order's sinful nature.

- That the form of confession that the Order practiced kept these sins within the confines of the group.

- That the Order financially profited by improper and immoral means and refused to give requisite alms and hospitality.

- That they conducted all their business in secret meetings and at night and that the above errors could only flourish because of this secrecy.[3]

FIG. 14.10. Satan calling forth His Legions (18th century). The immortal William Blake captures the essence of the frenzy of the charges made against the Order.

While the provincial councils pursued their nefarious efforts against individual Templars, the papal commission on the Order opened its first session in Paris on November 12, 1309, to consider the fate of the Order as a whole. The eight church dignitaries appointed as commissioners by Clement had all received Philip's approval. No one came forward to defend the Order. Philip's jailers, under whom all French Templars were imprisoned, were none too anxious to arrange transport and accommodations for the witnesses.

The first session of the papal commission ended on November 28, leaving Philip little cause for anxiety that the commission would be an effective forum for the Order to defend itself. The second session began on February 3, 1310. Philip ordered his jailers to be more cooperative in bringing forth those prisoners who wished to be witnesses. A group of fifteen Templars came forward to declare the Order's innocence. Suddenly a stampede followed, eventually growing to 597 brothers who offered to present testimony in the Order's defense. On March 28, four brothers were chosen as spokesmen for the group.

On March 31 and April 7, Pierre de Bologna made lengthy statements in which he vehemently denied all the charges. He explained that any confessions made by the brethren had been extracted under torture. He reminded the council that in countries where torture was illegal, virtually nothing was said against the Order. He accused the king and his henchmen of attacking the Order in a shameful vendetta of foul lies. He explained the pernicious effects of torture on the human psyche, stating that torture left its victims devoid of freedom of mind. Keeping the brethren jailed under royal custody, facing the continual threat of murder and torture, made a mockery of any semblance of justice. He objected to the presence of Philip's ministers at the ecclesiastical proceedings, as laymen were specifically prohibited from attending. He reminded the commissioners of the two centuries of service the Order had rendered to Christianity.

By May 1310, the situation had shifted in the Templars' favor for the first time in almost three years. Philip was forced to take another approach. He reopened a provincial ecclesiastical council near Paris on May 11, convened under the authority of another of his henchmen, the newly appointed archbishop of Sens, Phillipe de Marigny, brother of the powerful royal chamberlain. The very next day, May 12, Archbishop de Marigny declared fifty-four Templar brothers—who had just testified in defense of the Order before the papal commission—guilty as relapsed heretics because they had revoked earlier confessions made under torture. The men were immediately taken to a field and burned alive, heroically proclaiming their innocence and that of the Order as they died.

The impact of this atrocity silenced any future witnesses. Meanwhile, the burnings continued. Within days, 120 men perished by fire. The archbishops of Reims and Rouen, both Philip's appointees, began their own provincial councils. An uncounted number of Templars went to their deaths. Then it was discovered that Pierre de Bologna had mysteriously disappeared from jail; most probably murdered. The second session of the papal commission adjourned on May 30.

When the papal commission reconvened for its third and final session on November 3, 1310, only a handful of witnesses were found willing to testify in favor of the Order. On June 5, 1311, the papal commission rendered its findings to King Philip. A complete record of the hearings was prepared for the pope. The commission concluded that the case against the Order was

FIG. 14.11. Burning of the Templars (14th century). The provincial councils under the authority of bishops appointed by Philip made short work of those who defended the Order before the papal commission.

unproved. Evidence had been found, however, that unorthodox practices were taking place that should not go unpunished. This was enough for Philip.

On October 16, 1311, the general council of the Church, which had been delayed by a year, opened in Vienne, France. The ambitious council turned out to be very unpopular. One-third of the invited clergy failed to attend and none of the invited European royalty showed up. Clement's concern was clearly limited to the disposal of the Templar property. Clement also realized he earnestly needed more damaging evidence then had so far been collected. With the exception of France, home to Philip's gruesome machinery of state, there had been little confirming evidence of Order-wide guilt in the other European countries where trials and inquiries were also held.

Clement formally invited Templars to come and defend themselves. Nine Templars appeared at the council to plead for the Order, stating that fifteen hundred to two thousand brothers awaited the chance to testify on the Order's behalf. Church members in attendance, with the exception of the French clergy, wished to allow the defenders to testify before the council. Clement, however, ordered the immediate arrest of the small advance group to dissuade the others from coming forth.

Clement was unable to gain ascendancy over the council because of the transparency of his case. Philip, grew impatient. In February 1312, he sent a delegation to plead his concerns to Clement. In March, Philip issued an ultimatum stating that the Order must be suppressed because evidence of heresy and other crimes had been found in June by the papal commission.

On March 20, 1312, Philip arrived with a military force to ensure the action of the council. The matter was to be forever closed. On March 22, a secret consistory of the Council of Vienne was convened. Clement presented his bull *Vox in excelso* to the assembled cardinals and prelates. In it he stated that while the evidence against the Order did not justify its definitive condemnation, the proceedings had so scandalized the Order that no honorable man would consider membership. This state of affairs would so weaken the efforts of Christendom in the Holy Land that he was bound to abolish the Order. The consistory

voted by a four-fifths majority to suppress the Order. On April 3, Clement publicly read *Vox in excelso,* and the dissolution of the Knights Templar was complete. "It was done. It was so simple, Clement discovered, after all. In a few sentences and a few minutes he had succeeded where all the armies of Islam had failed."[4]

As might be expected, the Order's wealth had been systematically looted during the years since the first arrests. With conviction a foregone conclusion, charters granting property had been revoked. Stores of food, clothing, horses, livestock, movable property, and even timber had been confiscated by governments and the Church. Rents due the Order had been collected for years by the authorities. Debts payable to convicted heretics were absolved.

On May 6, 1312, Clement decreed in the bull *Considerantes dudum* that the fate of leaders of the Order would be dealt with by papal authority, while the brothers would submit to the provincial councils for judgment. Most surviving brothers were treated fairly gently. Those who were found innocent or submitted willingly to the Church were allowed to remain in former Templar houses and were even granted pensions from remaining Order property. Only those who refused to confess, or who revoked their confessions, were punished as heretics and burnt. Many brave knights chose this path.

The four ranking Templar leaders—Grand Master Jacques de Molay, Visitor of France Hugh de Pairaud, Preceptor of Normandy Geoffroi de Charney, and Preceptor of Aquitaine Geoffroi de Gonneville—were brought before a special papal commission in Paris on March 18, 1314. The hearing was to be a mere formality since the leaders had repeatedly confessed; all four were to be imprisoned for life. But de Molay and de Charney revoked their confessions and proclaimed the innocence of the Order. Thus guilty of a relapse into heresy, the two were turned over to the civil authorities for burning that very evening. With great courage, loudly proclaiming their innocence and orthodoxy, Jacques de Molay and Geoffroi de Charney were burned at the stake on Ile de Javiaux, a small island in the Seine. Their behavior was widely admired by the assembled onlookers, who reverently collected their ashes as relics.

Legends were immediately born that seemed

FIG. 14.12. The burning of Jacques de Molay and Geoffroi de Charney (14th century). At the end of all the confessions and recantations, the Grand Master and Preceptor of Normandy died the death of heroes and martyrs to their assertions of the Order's innocence.

Fig. 14.13. ABOVE: Ile de Javiaux and the scene of the execution of the Grand Master and Preceptor of Normandy. The plaque shown below right is visible in the center of the photo (Vere Chappell).

Fig. 14.14. BELOW LEFT: Commemorative sign (Vere Chappell).

Fig. 14.15. BELOW RIGHT: Detail of commemorative plaque (Vere Chappell).

to vindicate these once-great warriors against the injustices that had been perpetrated against them. It was said that a group of Templars who had proclaimed their innocence and were being taken to their executions passed by Guillaume de Nogaret. One screamed out a curse against the villainous lawyer: In eight days de Nogaret would appear before the tribunal of the Lord to face his judgment. Eight days later, de Nogaret died. Jacques de Molay is said to have uttered a curse as the flames engulfed him, demanding that if the Order were innocent, the pope be summoned to God's tribunal within forty days and the king within the year to answer for their crimes. Clement died in thirty-three days, Philip eight months later. Three of Philip's sons succeeded him to the throne. All were dead within fourteen years of Philip's demise, thus ending the three-hundred-year reign of the direct line of the Capetian royal family.

FIG. 14.16. Jacques de Molay (18th century).

CHAPTER 15

The Treasure of the Knights Templar

The inevitable question regarding the Knights Templar is, of course, were they guilty? I believe it should be rephrased: Of what might the Templars have been guilty, and who among them were?

Common sense must accompany any speculation on the question. The story of the Templars contains the entire spectrum of human experience: heroism and cowardice, generosity and greed, intelligence and stupidity, humility and pride, self-denial and self-indulgence, spiritual aspirations and failings, adherence to and betrayal of oaths. To help place these men in context, let us keep in mind that throughout the two hundred years of the Order's existence, the vast majority of its members were little removed from peasants, while most of its knights were far from the spiritual luminaries of myth. On the other hand, I believe that some Templars did live up to the elements of their myth.

It is impossible for anyone to state with certainty whether the Order was guilty or innocent of the charges leveled against it. The question will forever remain one of the vexing problems of history. Was there a policy of heresy—either passed along in a secret oral tradition widely available to the numerous preceptories throughout the world, or clutched tightly to the breast of each Grand Master and his chosen elite? This is exactly the type of conspiracy the French king and pope accused them of perpetrating. Many Templars died, facing torture and imprisonment,

FIG. 15.1. Manuscript page (13th century) from *Parzival* by Wolfram von Eschenbach (ca. 1170–ca. 1220). Parzival was the son of Gahmuret (Kamuret) an Angevin knight who traveled to the East and served the Baruch, the Caliph of Baghdad. He was first married to an African queen by whom he fathered Feirefiz, the piebald knight, the greatest warrior of the East. Parzival, destined to be the Grail king, was the greatest knight of the West. The Grail was guarded by the Knights Templar. It was the ultimate prize of the chivalric quest, "For whoever desires the Grail has to approach that prize with the sword."[1]

and the Order was ruined as a result of these accusations. Yet, the only conspiracy of which we have unmistakable evidence is that between King Philip, Pope Clement, and Counselor de Nogaret.

For centuries historians, occultists, conspiracy theorists, and others have speculated on the guilt or innocence of the Templars. The question has become a virtual litmus test, an article of faith, among opposing camps. Some believe that the Templars were the mystical harbingers of light and the secret initiators of the Renaissance and all later esoteric movements. Others believe the Order had degenerated into an evil and idolatrous sect, whose spiritual descendants still function as the cynical, atheistic, and nameless forces behind the international statist movement embodied by the United Nations and other prototypical world-government organizations. Still others assert the so-called "rationalist" position, the brightly polished intellectual suit of armor worn by the skeptical historian who essentially states that the Templars were indeed a part of the historical record and were exterminated in the Middle Ages. Those Templars who survived may have joined other religious orders or entered civilian life, but they eventually died out and were forgotten—except for periodic outbreaks of a kind of St. Vitus's dance of mythological passion, fueled alternately by romantics and charlatans. People of this mind-set point to the lack of tangible documentary evidence of either doctrinal heresy within the Order or the visibility of a "hidden tradition." They satisfy themselves that the cause of historical accuracy has been served by their refusal to see the larger thematic picture.

The scholarly creativity and sense of humor that historian and erotologist G. Legman brings to the discussion is unique. He writes that the Templars were exquisitely guilty as charged—they were a homosexual orgy cult based on Luciferian-dualist principles in which the mysteri-

ous idol, Baphomet, is the key. Legman appends the long section on the Templars from scholar-antiquarian Thomas Wright's 1866 essay "The Worship of the Generative Powers" in support of his conclusions. Both Legman and Wright trace the initiation ritual of which the Templars were accused through the Gnostic phallic worship of pre-Christian and anti-Christian cults. Wright ascribes the obscene rites described by early Christian heresiologists to "a mixture of the license of the vulgar Paganism of antiquity with the wild doctrines of the latter Eastern philosophers."[2] He believed that Persian Manichaeans fled persecutions in the east by migrating west and establishing sects of the nature of the Cathars. He further identifies the medieval Satan with Priapus.

The Gnostic model of the bisexual and androgynous nature of divinity has long been taken by various sects as an endorsement of both heterosexual and homosexual contact between adherents. The idea that the Templars were infused with an earlier broad-based sexual magical paganism—whose universality extends through Sufism, Buddhism, Hinduism, Kabbalistic Judaism, Taoism, the sixteenth-century witch cults, and the twentieth-century activities of Gerald Gardner and Aleister Crowley—may seem fanciful. Yet something like this is exactly what we are contemplating when acknowledging a heretical doctrine among the Templars that was not solely the creation of Philip and de Nogaret. To dispute this possibility entirely seems as perilous as embracing it wholeheartedly.

I believe the evidence points to an interpretation that neither exaggerates the realities of history and common sense nor sacrifices the mystery and romance that have accompanied the Templars since the day of their founding. Three critical influences are indisputable in this history, and

Fig. 15.2. Pan and Maenad. The erotic element of the charges against the Templars have led to much speculation on their veracity.

their effects must be accounted for in any discussion that seeks to accept the facts of human behavior as we know it.

The first factor was the doctrinal creativity employed by Saint Bernard in establishing the Rule of the Order, and the propaganda designed to attract members and financial backers. Bernard made use of a sophisticated interpretive methodology that tended to explore, examine, and create religious dogma. A military-religious order of knight-monks—a warrior clergy—was a new idea for Christianity. Its shadowy origins might easily be traced to the story of King David in the Old Testament, in which David's slaying of Goliath identifies him as a holy killer in the serv-ice of the Lord. Jesus often spoke as a warrior, using military analogies to express the unequivocal nature of the commitment required to progress along the spiritual path. When he said, "Think not that I have come to send peace on earth; I come not to send peace, but a sword,"[3] he eloquently expressed the necessity for unrelenting battle against the forces of darkness.

But the fact is that Bernard invented a new concept. It was elegant and alive. It fit the requirements of the social, political, and spiritual circumstances of the day perfectly. Yet it came at the tail end of a long period of cultural stagnation. That the full weight of the Church proved so receptive to Bernard's spiritual child may have

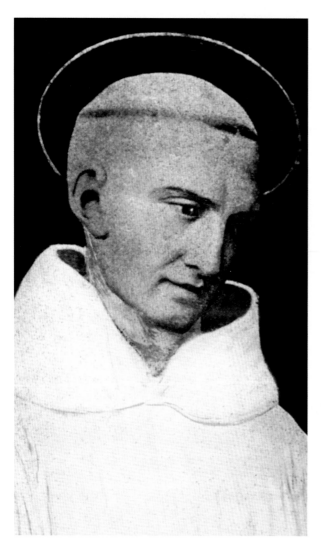

FIG. 15.3. St. Bernard (19th century). A man with a unique vision and a ready audience.

opened a gateway in an otherwise dormant European psyche. Kings and nobles joined their energies to this new idea. It was not science. It was theology. A magnificent change was introduced to European Christianity, and its originator was canonized for his efforts. On the other hand, the saint's spiritual children were to be anathematized and exterminated. What so clearly distinguished the Templars from the Hospitallers and the Teutonic Knights was the rarefied Templar myth. Their founding was a creative psychic act that briefly illumined medieval Europe; their destruction was a dark event of equal but opposite magnitude.

The second critical factor was the influence of contact with the Holy Land upon Europeans

FIG. 15.4. David slaying Goliath (12th century). The holy warrior wielding the sword of righteousness against the powers of evil is an idea with deep roots in Western culture.

FIG. 15.5. Jerusalem (12th century). A land of enchantment and myth, where God visited the earth in the flesh, and waged His war against the Powers of Darkness with the aid of His faithful comrades in arms.

in general, and members of the military orders in particular. Arab culture was infinitely more refined than that of Europe in the Dark Ages. The region was also replete with many other faiths. The mystics, fakirs, Zoroastrians, Gnostics, Sufis, and Buddhists whom they encountered would have presented a kaleidoscopic panorama to the newly arrived Crusaders. It was inevitable that the more intelligent and spiritually inclined knights would compare the superstitions and dogmas of Catholicism with the richness and sophistication of the Oriental theologies to which they were exposed. Increasing doubt concerning the exclusive possession of divine favor by Christianity would gradually undermine orthodoxy. The initial contact between Crusaders and the Assassins occurred as the latter were in the process of a systematic overturning of traditional Muslim beliefs. Some sense of the subtlety of this effort may have been communicated to their new acquaintances. The rejection of Islamic orthodoxy by the Assassin initiate is profoundly reminiscent of the rejection of Christian orthodoxy ascribed to the Templars by their accusers.[4]

The military orders were the most stable European presence among the varied Crusading entities. We have seen the local baronage, financially exhausted by the requirements of self-defense, donate land and fortresses to the orders. European kings and nobles came for a time of crusading and left to return home—undoubtedly

FIG. 15.7. Crusader canteen. This Arabic style design was manufactured by Crusaders in Palestine.

FIG. 15.6. Crusader and Muslim at chess (13th century). The two Templars shown in figure 2.15 on page 48 are here a Christian and Arab warrior. How close were the antagonists?

enriched by their experience—so that during the two centuries in question European society was certainly influenced by its contact with Outremer. But the military orders were a continuous presence. Members would learn the language, bargain and conduct business, enter personal friendships and political alliances, read literature, discourse on philosophy, and even quietly take lovers. In time, the ranks of the orders would contain people who had spent more of their lives in the East than in Europe, people more at home with oriental culture than with that of their birthplace.

The third factor that must be weighed into the Templar question is the influence of the Cathars. We repeatedly encounter the popularity and primacy of Languedoc in the history of the Templars. From the enthusiastic reception to their earliest promotional activities, to their despicable conduct during the Albigensian Crusades,

FIG. 15.8. OPPOSITE: Roquefixade town square (Vere Chappell). Is this in fact a Cathar version of the tantric lingam-yoni so common in Indian iconography?

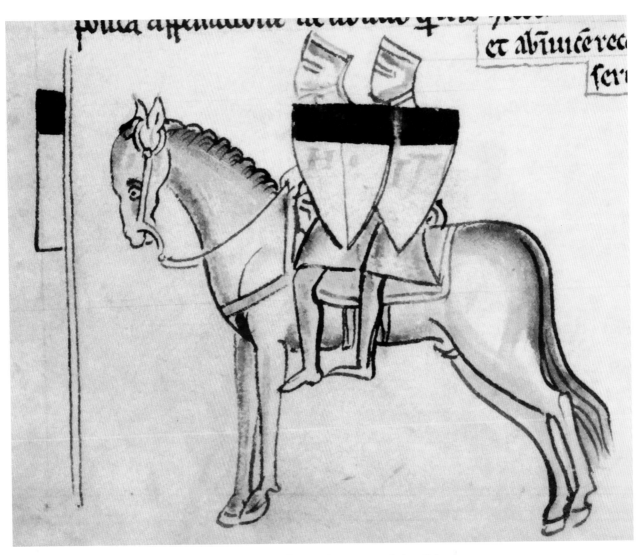

FIG. 15.9. The famed Templar seal celebrating the embrace of poverty and simplicity (13th century). The reader might pause again to hear the cries of innocence from the last Grand Master before drawing any final conclusions on heretical Templar doctrines.

Templar history is inextricably entwined with that of Languedoc. The very heresy they were enlisted to stamp out included elements with which they were accused during their own trials. If heresy did enter the Order, this was another likely area of ingress. For example, the sacred kiss of which the Templars were accused echoes the Cathar kiss of peace among the Perfect. The charge of spitting on the cross seems to be in line with the Cathar hatred of the image of the crucified Jesus. The term *bougre*, or *bugger*, used against the Cathars anticipates the charge of homosexuality against the Templars. The collective confession of the *apparellamentum* among the Perfect seems to be echoed in the Templar chapter proceedings. The rejection of family is common to both, as is their overtly antisexual attitude.

Antinomian Christianity would immediately choose the cross as a primary symbol to disparage in its quest for truth. The loathsome ideal of vicarious atonement, in which an innocent scapegoat is offered by the coward for his own spiritual redemption, could well be construed as worthy of disdain. Nor is it difficult to imagine the transformation of the Cathar rejection of the physical body and its sexual nature into an embrace of apparent licentiousness. In both responses to the psychobiological needs of the human being, there is an ascetic rejection of one aspect of the psyche—either the physical hunger for sex in the case of the celibate, or the emotional hunger for bonding and personalized affection in the case of the libertine.

We pause for a word of caution in support of the innocence of the Templars. It has been said that no Templar came forward to die for his heretical beliefs as so many Cathar martyrs did. Yet Jacques de Molay, for all his wavering, died a martyr proclaiming the innocence of the Order, as did many others who could have easily escaped the flames of the Inquisition if they had simply refused to revoke their confessions made under torture. For the esoteric student to blandly assume the guilt of the Templars to advance a romantic theory of history and initiation may well be to defile the Order's memory with the slanders of the French king. Charles Henry Lea points out that accepting the guilt of the Templars logically implies accepting the Inquisition's later accusations against the witches. He also makes the astute observation that if the Templars really were guilty of founding or promulgating an anti-Christian doctrine, *they would have concealed their heresy* with a carefully graded progressive unveiling of the secret. He dismisses as absurd the idea that any heresy would immediately be revealed to all and sundry at the first occasion of their admission to the Order.[5]

I would suggest that the influence of the spiritual creativity of Saint Bernard, the exposure to the rich and varied spiritual traditions of the Near East, and the continual effects of the heretical Cathar current created an inner corps of ini-

tiates within the Knights Templar who developed alternate doctrines of spiritual attainment. While there is no convincing evidence of a clandestine Rule that enjoined upon the Order the behavior of which it was accused, this underground elite, when exposed to the mystical tenets of the Assassins, would have found therein a spiritual richness worthy of their complete attention. And these adepts, some of whom survived, were the mystical channels by which the Gnostic-Ismaili legacy entered European occultism, where it has continued to influence the Western Mystery Tradition ever since. I would further suggest that this Spiritual Wisdom is the true identity of the much fabled Templar treasure.

FIG. 15.10. The Mystery remains, cloaked in Silence.

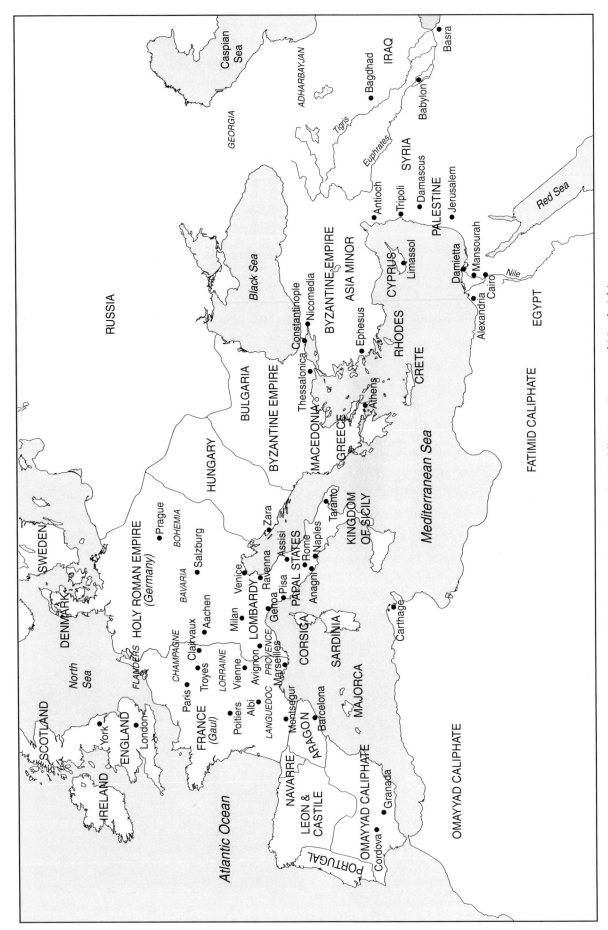

FIG. 15.11. Europe, Asia Minor, the Middle East, Egypt, and North Africa

FIG. 15.12. Castles, cities, regions, countries, and states of the Holy Land

Acknowledgments

There are two people without whom this book could never have happened. Stella Grey and Emma Gonzalez have put in so much effort in the area of art research and permissions that I can never thank either of them enough. Stella also contributed her critical editorial judgment at times when I had lost all perspective. Emma's aesthetic eye assisted with decisions on visual content. I am grateful for Stella's generosity and her demonstrated faith in this project. Emma served as the living embodiment of persistence, determination, and competence.

I thank Vere and Lita Chappell for sharing their privacy in the photo record of their European Templar quest. Steven Brooke, master photographer, has revealed the essence of the Holy Land in his exquisite images and provided me valuable technical guidance. The talented artist Paul Kirchner has brought to life some of the powerful Muslim warriors whose culture generally forbade contemporary portraits. Thanks to Dr. David Nicolle, a true scholar of the Crusades, for allowing me to use his photos. Thaedra MabraKhan's *Cristo Vino* electrifies this collection. My friend Martyn Hanson, a modern Templar indeed, helped with British research. Bill Breeze contributed rare artwork from the archives of O.T.O. Donald Weiser helped with research materials. Jennifer Belt of Art Resource extended the hand of friendship, and thereby made this project viable. Thanks to Ed Whitley of Bridgeman Art Library for his help when it did the most good. Cory Grace of the Freer Gallery of Art was particularly kind, as were Adi Engel of Albatross Aerial Photography, and my friend John Warren of Osprey Military. Dame Stella Bernardi of the Grand Priory of Knights Templar in England and Wales was generous with both her time and the Order's resources. Emma especially wanted to thank the staff at the Turkish Culture and Tourism Office in Los Angeles, along with Mert Icgoren, and Michael Murphy, who helped facilitate contact with the Topkapi Museum in Istanbul. Gill Cannell of Corpus Christi College in England, Lenaick Le Moigno of the Bibliothèque Nationale in France, and Jorge Descalzo of the Patrimonio Nacional in Spain went out of their way to help her.

Works by scholars such as Malcolm Barber, Helen Nicholson, J. M. Upton-Ward, Jonathan Riley-Smith, Steven Runciman, Farhad Daftary, Marshall Hodgson, and Malcolm Lambert were particularly useful, as were illustrated collections by Peter Coss and Malcolm Billings.

I thank my wife and family for their love and patience as I dwelt in the realms of obsession. Kind words and smiles were too often overshadowed by the flames of the creative fire into which I was plunged.

Jon Graham has once again earned my thanks for his incredible breadth of spirit and intellect. Jeanie Levitan inhabits the top tier of the heavenly host of publishing professionals. Knowing Ehud Sperling for some three and a half decades, it's hard to imagine life without his brilliance, dedication, and the confidence he has more than once extended to me.

I must finally acknowledge the fact that Osama bin Laden and his minions have made absolutely clear that we are once again fully immersed in the Crusades. I hope the history presented here will help gird the loins of the West for that which must follow.

NOTES TO THE TEXT

Quotation on page 7 is taken from Saint Bernard's letter to Hughes de Payens, ca. 1135, "In Praise of the New Knighthood," translated by Lisa Coffin in *The Templars and the Assassins: The Militia of Heaven*, by James Wasserman (Rochester: Destiny Books, 2001).

Introduction

[1] Remarks by President Bush upon arrival on the South Lawn on September 16, 2001, "This crusade, this war on terrorism is going to take a while. And the American people must be patient."

[2] Al-Qaeda, founded in 1998, is technically known as the World Islamic Front for Jihad Against Jews and Christians. See "September 11, 2001 Remembered," in *The Slaves Shall Serve: Meditations on Liberty*, James Wasserman (New York: Sekmet Books, 2004).

[3] This precept is still in force. Describing bin Laden's change of heart toward the United States, reporter James Risen wrote, "Finally he turned completely against the United States with the onset of the Persian Gulf crisis . . . in 1990. He saw the presence of hundreds of thousands of American and other foreign troops on Saudi soil as a deep religious affront—the return of the barbarian Crusaders to defile Islam's holy places." (*New York Times*, September 6, 1998).

Chapter 1 The First Crusade and Victory

[1] Steven Runciman, *A History of the Crusades*, 3 vols. (1951; reprint, London: The Folio Society, 1994), vol. 1, p. 140.

Chapter 2 The Knights Templar Order

[1] Quoted by Norman Cantor, *The Civilization of the Middle Ages* (New York: Harper Perennial, 1994), p. 34.

[2] J. M. Upton-Ward, *The Rule of the Templars* (Suffolk: The Boydell Press, 1992), p. 19.

[3] Ibid., p. 19.

[4] Edward Burman, *The Templars: Knights of God* (Wellingborough: Aquarian Press, 1986), p. 30.

[5] Upton-Ward, *The Rule of the Templars*, p. 87.

[6] In 1877, a forged "Secret Rule" of the Templars was published by the German Mason Merzdorf. He pretended it was a recently discovered thirteenth-century manuscript that proved the Templar heresy, including alliance with the Cathars, defiling the cross, worship of Baphomet, the obscene kiss, ceremonial readings from the Koran, and so on. See Peter Partner, *The Murdered Magicians: The Templars and Their Myth* (Oxford: Oxford University Press, 1981), pp. 161–63.

[7] Upton-Ward, *The Rule of the Templars*, p. 79.

[8] Ibid., p. 112.

[9] "In Praise of the New Knighthood," in Wasserman, *The Templars and the Assassins*, p. 279.

[10] Ibid., p. 278.

[11] Ibid., p. 280.

[12] Ibid., p. 278.

[13] Ibid., p. 283.

[14] Henry Charles Lea, *A History of the Inquisition of the Middle Ages*, 3 vols. (1888; reprint, New York: Russell & Russell, 1955), vol. 3, pp. 250–51.

[15] Burman, *The Templars*, p. 80.

Chapter 3 The Growth of the Knights Templar

[1] This particular privilege was to become problematic in later years as corruption tainted the Order. Excommunicated nobles paid to be admitted to membership upon their deathbeds so they could be buried in consecrated Christian ground, effectively circumventing one of the worst consequences of excommunication.

Chapter 4 The Second Crusade and the Syrian Assassins

[1] Marco Polo's account became the model for an Arabic novel, written in 1430, that has been mistakenly identified as a source of Polo's tale. (See Joseph von Hammer-Purgstall, *The History of the Assassins* [1835; reprint, New York: Burt Franklin, 1968], p. 136, and Farhad Daftary, *The Assassin Legends* [London: I. B. Tauris & Company, 1995], pp. 118–20.) Polo's book remained the most popular source for the Assassin myth for over four hundred years.

[2] Curiously, if Hammer-Purgstall is accurate, these were the same colors worn by the Assassin *fidais*. He ascribes white to innocence and devotion and red to blood and murder. See *The Assassins*, p. 56.

Chapter 5 The Rise of Saladin

[1] Barber, *The New Knighthood* (Cambridge: Cambridge University Press, 1994), p. 89.

2 Daftary, *The Assassin Legends*, pp. 68 and 71; Daftary, *The Ismailis: Their History and Doctrines* (Cambridge: Cambridge University Press, 1994), p. 398.

3 Bernard Lewis, *The Assassins: A Radical Sect in Islam* (New York: Basic Books, 1968), pp. 116–17.

4 Stephen Howarth, *The Knights Templar* (London: Collins, 1982), p. 145.

5 "In Praise of the New Knighthood," in Wasserman, *The Templars and the Assassins*, p. 285. This apologia for Gérard's actions was suggested by Malcolm Barber in *The New Knighthood*, p. 181.

Chapter 8 The Albigensian Heresy

1 Malcolm Lambert, *The Cathars* (Oxford: Blackwell Publishers, 1998), pp. 43–44.

2 Ibid., p. 21.

3 Joseph R. Strayer, *The Albigensian Crusades* (Ann Arbor: University of Michigan Press, 1992), pp. 143–50, provides extracts of Cathar rituals.

4 KJV, Matt. 3:11; see also Acts 1:5.

5 Lambert, *The Cathars*, p. 69.

6 Strayer, *The Albigensian Crusades*, p. 75.

7 A highly recommended study of European Christian heretical sects from the eleventh through sixteenth centuries is Norman Cohn, *The Pursuit of the Millenium*, 3rd ed. (New York: Oxford University Press, 1970).

8 KJV, 2 Timothy 2:19, and Numbers 16:5. These two biblical verses are offered in support of the historicity of the legate's statement by Malcolm Lambert in *The Cathars*, p. 103.

Chapter 9 The Fifth Crusade and Saint Francis

1 Malcolm Barber, on the other hand, says it was returned. See *The New Knighthood*, p. 130.

Chapter 11 The Seventh Crusade and Baybars

1 Christopher Marshall, *Warfare in the Latin East, 1192–1291* (Cambridge: Cambridge University Press, 1992), p. 41, quoting from the contemporary account in the Rothelin manuscript, *Continuation de Guillaume de Tyr de 1229 à 1261.*

2 John J. Robinson, *Born in Blood* (New York: M. Evans & Co., 1989), p. 60.

Chapter 13 The Templars in Defeat

1 Barber, *The New Knighthood*, p. 1.

2 To help place Philip's treatment of Boniface in context: In 878, Pope John VIII had been imprisoned and starved by a nobleman who sought papal sanction for a candidate he proposed as Holy Roman Emperor. In 897, Pope Stephen VI had the corpse of his predecessor exhumed, robed, and tried before an ecclesiastic council, where it was found guilty, stripped, mutilated, and flung into the Tiber. A revolt in Rome the same year resulted in Stephen being imprisoned and strangled in his cell. A century later, Otto I, king of Germany and Holy Roman Emperor, deposed Pope John XVI, gouged out his eyes, cut off his tongue, and paraded him through the streets of Rome turned backward on an ass. In 1052, Pope Leo IX was imprisoned for nine months. As late as 1075, Pope Gregory VII was physically attacked while celebrating Christmas Mass and carried off by agents of a Roman nobleman.

Chapter 14 Arrest and Trial

1 G. Legman, *The Guilt of the Templars* (New York: Basic Books, 1966), p. 16.

2 Ibid., p. 94.

3 Legman has pointed out that what makes these charges interesting is their encyclopedic nature. If Philip and de Nogaret wished solely to destroy the Order, the charges of denying Christ and defiling the cross would have been sufficient to condemn them to death. He also questions why some of the contemporary boilerplate accusations, such as bewitching cattle, murdering children, planning to assassinate the king, usury, and financial fraud were missing. See *The Guilt of the Templars*, p. 42.

4 Howarth, *The Knights Templar*, p. 305.

Chapter 15 The Treasure of the Knights Templar

1 CAPTION NOTE: *Parzival* by Wolfram von Eschenbach, translated by Helen M. Mustard and Charles E. Passage, (New York: Vintage Books, 1961) p. 269.

2 Thomas Wright, "The Worship of the Generative Powers," in *A Discourse on the Worship of Priapus*, Richard Payne Knight (1865; reprinted as *Sexual Symbolism, A History of Phallic Worship* [New York: The Julian Press, 1961]), p. 106.

3 KJV, Matt. 10:34.

4 See discussion of the *Qiyama* in Wasserman, *The Templars and the Assassins*, pp. 116–20.

5 Lea, *A History of the Inquisition of the Middle Ages*, vol. 3, p. 268.

PHOTO CREDITS

All chapter decorations: Stained glass window with Templar Seal. La Couvertoirade, France. Photo by Vere Chappell.

Frontispiece: Rider on the White Horse, ca. 1310–ca. 1325. From the *Apocalypse*. Roy. 19. B.XV. Folio No: 37 (detail). © The British Library. Photo Credit: HIP/Art Resource, NY.

Introduction

I.1 Painting by Dominique Papety, (1815–1849) Salon of 1845. Inv.: MV 402. Photo: Gérard Blot. Chateaux de Versailles et de Trianon, Versailles, France Photo Credit: Réunion des Musées Nationaux/Art Resource, NY.

I.2 Mosaic from cupola. Baptistry, Florence, Italy. Photo Credit: Erich Lessing/Art Resource.

I.3 Training in Knightly Skills, MS 264, fol. 82v., Bodleian Library, London

I.4 The Jousts of St. Inglevert. 1390, Harley 4379. Folio No: 23v. Min. British Library, London. Photo Credit: HIP/Art Resource, NY.

I.5 From a Latin psalter compiled for Westminster Abbey ca. 1175–ca. 1200. Royal 2. A. XXII. Folio No: 220. British Library, London. Photo Credit: HIP/Art Resource, NY.

I.6 From a manuscript of *Le Roman de Lancelot du Lac*. The Pierpont Morgan Library, New York, MS 806, f. 262.

I.7 Devils seizing the soul of a knight at a tournament. MS Royal 19 C I fol. 204v. British Library, London.

I.8 From *History of the World*, Volume 3, by John Clark Ridpath.

I.9 From *History of the World*, Volume 3, by John Clark Ridpath.

I.10 From *The History of the Siege Jerusalem*, ms. fr. 2629 fol. 171, 1470. Bibliotheque Nationale, Paris. Photo Credit: Giraudon/Art Resource, NY.

I.11 From *Les Voyages d'Outremer*. France, 15th CE. Ms. fr. 9087, f. 85v. Bibliotheque Nationale, Paris. Photo Credit: Snark/Art Resource, NY.

I.21 Mosaic in the south gallery, 12th century. Hagia Sophia, Istanbul, Turkey. Photo Credit: Erich Lessing/Art Resource, NY.

I.22 *Codex Justinianus; Institutes, descriptio terrae sanctae*. Italian. 14th century. Biblioteca Capitolare, Padua, Italy Photo Credit: Erich Lessing/Art Resource, NY.

Chapter 1: The First Crusade

1.1 Miniature from the *Roman de Godefroi de Bouillon*. 1337. Ms. fr. 22495, fol. 15. Bibliotheque Nationale, Paris. Photo Credit: Giraudon/Art Resource, NY.

1.2 From *Abreviamen de las Estorias; a summary of Universal History, from the creation of the world to the death of the Emperor Henry VII*. Eger. 1500. Folio No: 45v. British Library, London. Photo Credit: HIP/Art Resource, NY.

1.3 From *History of the World*, Volume 3, by John Clark Ridpath.

1.4 From Guillaume de Tyr (c.1130–85) (vellum) Fr. 2630 f. 22v. Bibliotheque Nationale, Paris.

1.5 William of Tyre, *Histoire d'Outremer*, MS Yates Thompson 12 fol. 29. The British Library.

1.6 Ms. fr. 352, f. 62. Bibliotheque Nationale, Paris. Photo Credit: Snark/Art Resource, NY.

1.7 From *The Crusades of Godefroy de Bouillon*. Fr 9084 f. 20v. Bibliotheque Nationale, Paris. Bridgeman Art Library.

Chapter 2: The Knights Templar Order

2.1 Painting by Henri Charles Lehmann, (1814–1882) 1841. Chateaux de Versailles et de Trianon, Versailles, France. Photo Credit: Réunion des Musées Nationaux/Art Resource, NY.

2.2 Photo by Antiqua, Inc. Woodland Hills, CA.

2.7 Detail of the virgins traveling to Rome from the altarpiece of the Martyrdom and Execution of St. Ursula, in the sacristy (mural painting) by the Master of the Conquest of Mallorca. Basilica de San Francesco, Mallorca, Spain. Bridgeman Art Library.

2.8 Painting by Jean Fouquet, (c.1415/20–1481). From *Le Livre d'Heures d'Etienne Chevalier, The Suffrage of the Saints*. Ms 71 ; fol. 39. Photo: R. G. Ojeda. Musee de la Ville de Paris, Musee Carnavalet, Paris, France Photo Credit: Réunion des Musées Nationaux/Art Resource, NY.

2.10 Painting by Francois Marius Granet (1775–1849). Chateaux de Versailles et de Trianon, Versailles, France Photo Credit: Réunion des Musées Nationaux/Art Resource, NY.

2.11 Matthew Paris's sketch from his *Historia Anglorum*. Ref.: BM Royal MS. 14 C vii f. 42v. © The British Library.

2.12 Fresco. S. Bevignate, Perugia, Italy. Photo Credit: Alinari/Regione Umbria/Art Resource, NY.

2.13 Painting of St. Benedict, Anonymous, 11th century. S. Crisogono, Rome, Italy Photo Credit: Scala/Art Resource, NY.

2.15 From a manuscript of Alfonso X of Castile's *Libro de Ajedrez, dados y tables.* Biblioteca del Monasterio de Le Escorial, Madrid, Spain. Ref.: MS. T. 1. I 6, fol. 25. © Patrimonio Nacional, Spain.

2.16 Cathedral St. Lazare, Autun, France. 12th century. Photo Credit: Foto Marburg/Art Resource, NY.

2.17 From the *Luttrell Psalter.* Ca. 1300–ca.1340. Add. 42130. Folio No: 202v. Min. British Library, London. Photo Credit: HIP/Art Resource, NY.

2.18 From an English *Apocalypse,* ca. 1270 Bodleian Library, Ms. Douce 180 f. 88, Oxford.

2.19 Scene from I Sam. XXX:16–19. France (probably Paris), ca.1250 CE. MS. M.638, f. 34v. The Pierpont Morgan Library, NY. Photo Credit: The Pierpont Morgan Library/Art Resource, NY.

2.20 Scene from I Sam. XVII:20–22. MS. 638 fo. 27v. The Pierpont Morgan Library, NY. Photo Credit: The Pierpont Morgan Library/Art Resource, NY.

2.21 Cover of *Templar Inquest Book,* 1185. Ref.: PRO. Miscellaneous Books, series 1 E. 164, Number 16. © Public Record Office, London.

2.22 Initial C, 13th century. Sloane. 2435. Folio No. 85. Min. British Library, London. Photo Credit: HIP/Art Resource, NY.

Chapter 3: The Growth of the Knights Templar

3.10 Illumination by Basil. Latin Kingdom of Jerusalem ca. 1113–43. BL. MS Egerton 1139, fo. 12v. The British Library.

3.11 From *Universal History* of William of Tyre, Acre ca. 1284 AD. Bibliothèque Nationale, Paris. MS. Fr. 9084, f. 182v.

3.17 Reproduced by permission of Osprey Publishing, Men-at-Arms #155: *Knights of Christ,* Osprey Publishing. www.ospreypublishing.com.

Chapter 4: The Second Crusade and the Syrian Assassins

4.1 From *History of the Order of Assassins,* Enno Franzius, Funk & Wagnalls, 1969.

4.2 Illustration on vellum by Boucicaut Master, (fl. 1390–1430) (and workshop) Ms. Fr. 2810 f. 17. Bibliotheque Nationale, Paris. Bridgeman Art Library.

4.3 From *Jami al-Tavarikh,* by Rashid al-Din, MS Treasury 1653, fol. 360v. Persian, early 14th century. Topkapi Saray Museum, Istanbul.

4.4 Miniature from the *Roman de Godefroi de Bouillon,* 1337. Ms. Fr. 22495, f. 235v. Bibliotheque Nationale, Paris. Photo Credit: Snark/Art Resource, NY.

4.5 From the 15th century manuscript *Les passages d' Outremer.* Bibliotheque Nationale, Paris. Photo Credit: Snark/Art Resource, NY.

4.6 Painting by Francois-Marius Granet, (1775–1849). 1844 (oil on canvas). Chateau de Versailles, France. Lauros/Giraudon. Bridgeman Art Library.

4.7 From William of Tyre, *Histoire de Jérusalem,* MS 9087, fo. 206. Latin Kingdom of Jerusalem. ca. 1250. Photo Giraudon, Paris. Bridgeman Art Library.

4.10 How Lord John of Acre Was Keeping Watch on Some Saracens Who Requested Baptism. 1325–1330. Roy. 16.G.VI, fol. 101 v © British Library. Photo Credit: Erich Lessing/Art Resource, NY.

Chapter 5: The Rise of Saladin

5.2 After a contemporary miniature ca. 1180. Ann Ronan Picture Library, London. Photo Credit: HIP/Art Resource, NY.

5.4 Miniature from the *Roman de Godefroi de Bouillon.* 1337. Ms. fr. 22495, fol. 229. Bibliotheque Nationale, Paris, France, Photo Credit: Giraudon/Art Resource, NY.

5.5 Miniature from ms of Jacquemark Giélée's *Renart le Nouvel* (1289). Bibliothèque Nationale MS Fr. 371 f. 59; © Bibliothèque Nationale.

5.6 Photo Credit: Erich Lessing/Art Resource, NY.

5.7 From Matthew Paris's *Chronica Majora.* Cambridge, Corpus Christi College MS. 26, page 279 [140] bottom right margin. © The Master and Fellows of Corpus Christi College, Cambridge.

5.8 *Passages Faits Outremer* by Sébastien Mamerot. Ms. Fr. 5594 f. 197. Bibliothèque Nationale, Paris.

Chapter 6: The Third Crusade and Richard the Lionhearted

6.1 Tombs of the Plantagenet Kings. Colored stone. 13th century. Fontevrault, France. Photo Credit: Erich Lessing/Art Resource, NY.

6.2 Engraving by A. Sandoz, in *Illustrated History of England,* by John Cassell. Mary Evans Picture Gallery.

6.3 From *Chroniques de France ou de Saint Denis.* British Library, London. Photo Credit: Erich Lessing/ Art Resource, NY.

6.4 Detail from a page of Latin text from the *Luttrell Psalter*. ca. 1300– ca. 1340. Add. 42130. Folio No: 82. Min. (L). British Library, London. Photo Credit: HIP/Art Resource, NY.

Chapter 7: The Byzantine Crusade

7.1 From *Chroniques de France ou de Saint Denis*, ca. 1325–ca. 1350. British Library, London. Photo Credit: HIP/Art Resource, NY.

7.2 Painting by Domenico Tintoretto (1560–1635). Palazzo Ducale, Venice, Italy. Photo Credit: Erich Lessing/Art Resource, NY.

7.3 Painting by Eugene Delacroix (1798–1863). Louvre, Paris. Photo Credit: Erich Lessing/Art Resource, NY.

Chapter 8: The Albigensian Heresy

8.4 Illustration of an instruction to monks by abbot Johannes Klimax (6th century). 12th century icon. St. Catherine Monastery, Mount Sinai, Sinai Desert, Egypt. Photo Credit: Erich Lessing/Art Resource, NY.

8.7 *Psalter* of Henry of Blois. British Library, London. Photo credit: HIP/Art Resource, NY.

8.9 From *Chroniques de France ou de Saint Denis*, ca. 1325–ca. 1350. British Library, London. Photo Credit: HIP/Art Resource, NY.

8.10 Expulsion of the Albigensians, ca. 1300–ca. 1400. British Library, London. Photo Credit: HIP/Art Resource, NY.

Chapter 9: The Fifth Crusade and Saint Francis

9.1 Photo from Albatross Aerial Photography.

9.2 Painting by Benozzo Gozzoli (1420–1497). S. Francesco, Montefalco, Italy. Photo Credit: Scala/Art Resource, NY.

9.3 Matthew Paris's *Chronica Majora*. Ms 16 Roll 178. Cambridge, Corpus Christi College MS. 16, fol. 54v: © The Master and Fellows of Corpus Christi College, Cambridge. Bridgeman Art Library.

9.4 Early 14th century manuscript. BL MS. Add. 102929. fol 81v. © The British Library, London. Bridgeman Art Library.

Chapter 10: The Sixth Crusade and Frederick II

10.1 Biblioteca Apostolica Vaticana, The Vatican, Italy. Bridgeman Art Library.

10.2 Photo from Albatross Aerial Photography.

10.3 12th century fresco. Ancienne Chapelle des Templiers, Cressac, France. Photo Credit: Giraudon/Art Resource, NY.

10.4 Battle between Christians, from *History of the World*, Volume 3, by John Clark Ridpath.

10.5 From Matthew Paris's *Chronica Majora*. Cambridge, Corpus Christi College MS. 16, fol. 133v.

10.6 From Matthew Paris's *Chronica Majora*. Cambridge, Corpus Christi College MS. 16, fo. 170v. © The Master and Fellows of Corpus Christi College, Cambridge.

Chapter 11: The Seventh Crusade and Baybars

11.1 *The Book of the Faiz Monseigneur Saint Louis.* Photo Credit: Snark/Art Resource, NY.

11.2 King Louis IX. © The British Library, London. Bridgeman Art Library.

11.3 From *Chroniques de France ou de St. Denis*, ca. 1325–ca. 1350. Roy. 16.G.VI. Folio: 409v. [detail]. British Library, London. Photo Credit: HIP/Art Resource, NY.

11.4 *Livre des Faits de Monseigneur Saint Louis.* Ms Fr. 2829, f. 36v. Bibliothèque Nationale, Paris.

11.5 Early 15th century. Louvre, Paris. Photo Credit: Giraudon/Art Resource, NY.

11.6 Illuminated manuscript page from *Jami al-Tawarikh (Universal History)*, by Rashid al-Din. Iran, Tabriz, ca. 1330. Inv. Diez A, folio 70. S. 22. Photo: Ellwardt. Oriental Division. Staatsbibliothek zu Berlin, Berlin, Germany. Photo Credit: Bildarchiv Preussischer Kulturbesitz/Art Resource, NY.

11.7 China, Ming dynasty. Victoria and Albert Museum, London. Photo Credit: Art Resource, NY.

11.8 Ms. Sup. Pers. 1113. f. 180v–181. Bibliotheque Nationale, Paris. Bridgeman Art Library.

Chapter 12: The Eighth and Final Crusade

12.1 British Library, London. Photo Credit: HIP/Art Resource, NY.

12.2 From a book by Rashid-al-Din (1247–1318) (gouache) by Persian School, (14th century) Ms Pers.113 f.49. Bibliotheque Nationale, Paris, France, Bridgeman Art Library.

12.3 A battle between the forces of Naudar and Afrasiyab, from a *Shahnama (Book of Kings)* by Firdawsi, early 14th century, Il-Khanid dynasty, Opaque watercolor, ink, and gold on paper. Probably Iran. Freer Gallery of Art, Smithsonian Institution, Washington D.C.: Purchase F1929.36.

12.4 From *Chroniques de France ou de St. Denis*, 1375–1400. Roy. 20. C. VII, fol. 24 v. British Library, London. Photo Credit: Erich Lessing/Art Resource, NY.

Chapter 13: The Templars in Defeat

13.1 Engraving by Ghevauchet, French School, 19th century, Private Collection. Roger-Viollet, Paris, Bridgeman Art Library.

13.2 Painting by Karl Friedrich Lessing, (1808–1880). Rheinisches Landesmuseum, Bonn, Germany. Photo Credit: Erich Lessing/Art Resource, NY.

13.3 Medieval illustration for a 5th century late Roman manuscript. Art Museum of Barcelona. Palau Nacional, Parc de Montjuic.

13.4 The Pilgrimage of Raymond Lull, from Thomas le Muyesier, *Breviculum ex artbus Raimundi Lulli elctrum*, St. Petersberg. 92 fo. IV. Spanish ca. 1321. Badische Landesbibliothek.

13.5 From *Cronica Breve de Re di Francis*. BM Object Number 1871, 0812. 4427. British Museum, London.

13.6 Arnolfo di Cambio (ca. 1245–1302). Photo Credit: Scala/Art Resource, NY.

13.7 *Cronica Breve de Re di Francis*. BM Object Number 1870, 0514. 155. British Museum, London.

13.9 Engraving by French School, 19th century. Private Collection, Ken Welsh. Bridgeman Art Library.

Chapter 14: Arrest and Trial

14.1 *Chronicle of France or of St Denis*, 14th century. BL. Roy 20 C VII f. 42v British Library. Bridgeman Art Library.

14.3 From *The Scarlet Book of Freemasonry*, by M.W. Redding, Redding & Co. Masonic Publishers.

14.4 From *The Scarlet Book of Freemasonry*, by M.W. Redding, Redding & Co. Masonic Publishers.

14.5 Templar Initiation, courtesy Michael Moynihan and Jon Graham.

14.6 Illustration by Éliphas Lévi, *Transcendental Magic*, Rider & Company, London.

14.7 Painting (1491) by Vittore Carpaccio (1455–1525). Accademia, Venice, Italy. Photo Credit: Cameraphoto/Art Resource, NY.

14.8 Painting (1851) by Eugenio Lucas, (1827–1870). Photo: Herve Lewandowski. Louvre, Paris. Photo Credit: Réunion des Musées Nationaux/Art Resource, NY.

14.9 Painting by Pedro Berruguete. Museo del Prado, Madrid, Spain. Photo Credit: Erich Lessing/Art Resource, NY.

14.10 Painting by William Blake (1757–1827). Petworth House, Petworth, Sussex, Great Britain. Photo Credit: National Trust/Art Resource, NY.

14.11 From the *Chroniques de France ou de St. Denis*, ca. 1375–ca. 1400. Roy. 20. C. VII. Folio: 44v. Min. British Library, London. Photo Credit: HIP/Art Resource, NY.

14.12 From *Chroniques de France ou de St. Denis*, ca. 1375–ca. 1400. Roy. 20.C.VII. Folio: 48.Min. British Library, London. Photo Credit: HIP/Art Resource, NY.

14.16 From *Secret Societies of the Middle Ages*, by Thomas Keightley.

Chapter 15: The Templar Treasure

15.1 Banquet at the Grail Castle. ABOVE: Parzifal receiving the Grail. CENTER: Parzifal and his wife Condwiramurs on horseback. BELOW: After his baptism Feirefiz is allowed to see the Grail. Staatsbibliothek zu Berlin, Berlin. Photo Credit: Bildarchiv Preussischer Kulturbesitz/Art Resource, NY.

15.2 Pan and Maenad (detail). Museo Eoliano, Lipari, Italy. Photo Credit: Scala/Art Resource, NY.

15.3 From *The Life and Teaching of St. Bernard*, Andrew J. Luddy, M. H. Gill & Son, Ltd.

15.4 Combat between David and Goliath/David with head of Goliath. Single leaf. England, Winchester, Cathedral Priory of St. Swithin, ca. 1160–1180. MS. M. 619, verso. The Pierpont Morgan Library, New York. Photo: The Pierpont Morgan Library/Art Resource, NY.

15.5 12th Century map of Jerusalem. Below St. George assists the Christians. MS. 76 F 5, fol 1r © The Hague, Koninklijle Bibliotheek.

15.6 From a manuscript of Alfonso X of Castile's *Libro de Ajedrez, dados y tables*. Biblioteca del Monasterio de Le Escorial, Madrid, Spain. Ref.: MS. T. 1. I 6, fol. 25. © Patrimonio Nacional, Spain. Bridgeman Art Library.

15.7 Canteen. Probably Syria, mid-13th century. The large canteen recalls the shape of ceramic pilgrim flasks. Includes a representation of Virgin and Child and scenes from the life of Christ. Brass inlaid with silver. Freer Gallery of Art, Smithsonian Institution, Washington D.C.: Purchase F1941.10.

15.9 Matthew Paris's drawing from his *Chronica Majora*, Corpus Christi College MS 26, p 220. © The Masters and Fellows of Corpus Christi College, Cambridge.

15.10 The Silent Watcher, *The Equinox* I, 1, Courtesy Ordo Templi Orientis.

15.11 Map of Europe & Mediterranean, from *The Templars and the Assassins*, by James Wasserman, Inner Traditions.

15.12 Map of the Holy Land, from *The Templars and the Assassins*, by James Wasserman, Inner Traditions.

BIBLIOGRAPHY

Barber, Malcolm. *The New Knighthood*. Cambridge: Cambridge University Press, 1994.

———. *The Trial of the Templars*. Cambridge: Cambridge University Press, 1978.

Billings, Malcolm. *The Cross and the Crescent*. New York: Sterling Publishing, 1990.

Brooke, Steven. *Views of Jerusalem and the Holy Land*. New York: Rizzoli, 1998, and revised paperback, 2002.

———. *Views of Rome*. New York: Rizzoli, 1995.

Burman, Edward. *The Assassins: Holy Killers of Islam*. Wellingborough: Aquarian Press, 1987.

———. *The Templars: Knights of God*. Wellingborough: Aquarian Press, 1986.

Cantor, Norman F. *The Civilization of the Middle Ages*. New York: Harper Perennial, 1994.

Cohn, Norman. *The Pursuit of the Millennium*. 3rd ed. New York: Oxford University Press, 1970.

Coss, Peter. *The Knight in Medieval England 1000–1400*. Conshohocken, PA: Combined Books, 1993.

Daftary, Farhad. *The Assassin Legends*. London: I. B. Tauris & Company, 1995.

———. *The Ismailis: Their History and Doctrines*. Cambridge: Cambridge University Press, 1994.

———, ed. *Medieval Ismaili History and Thought*. Cambridge: Cambridge University Press, 1996.

De Lacy, O'Leary. *A Short History of the Fatimid Khalifate*. 1923. Reprint, Delhi: Renaissance Publishing House, 1987.

Durant, Will. *The Age of Faith*. Vol. 4 of *The Story of Civilization*. New York: Simon and Schuster, 1944.

———. *Caesar and Christ*. Vol. 3 of *The Story of Civilization*. New York: Simon and Schuster, 1950.

Eschenbach, Wolfram von. *Parzival*. Trans. with introduction by Helen M. Mustard and Charles E. Passage. New York: Vintage Books, 1961.

Franzius, Enno. *The History of the Order of the Assassins*. New York: Funk & Wagnalls, 1969.

Hammer-Purgstall, Joseph von. *The History of the Assassins*. 1835. Reprint, New York: Burt Franklin, 1968.

Hodgson, Marshall G. S. *The Order of Assassins*. The Hague: Mouton, 1955.

Howarth, Stephen. *The Knights Templar*. London: Collins, 1982.

Hutchet, Patrick, *Les Templiers: De la gloire à la tragédie*. Rennes: Editions Ouest-France, 2002.

Keightley, Thomas. *Secret Societies of the Middle Ages*. 1837. Reprint, Boston: Weiser Books, 2005.

Khayyam, Omar. *The Rubaiyat*. Trans. and ed. Edward Fitzgerald. New York: Collier Books, 1962.

Knight, Richard Payne and Thomas Wright. *A Discourse on the Worship of Priapus*. 1865. Reprinted as *Sexual Symbolism, A History of Phallic Worship*. New York: The Julian Press, 1961.

Lambert, Malcolm. *The Cathars*. Oxford: Blackwell Publishers, 1998.

Lea, Henry Charles. *A History of the Inquisition of the Middle Ages*. 3 vols. 1888. Reprint, New York: Russell & Russell, 1955.

Legman, G. *The Guilt of the Templars*. New York: Basic Books, 1966.

Lewis, Bernard. *The Assassins: A Radical Sect in Islam*. New York: Basic Books, 1968.

———. *The Crisis of Islam: Holy War and Unholy Terror*. New York: The Modern Library, 2003.

Lings, Martin. *Muhammad: His Life Based on the Earliest Sources*. New York: Inner Traditions, 1983.

Marshall, Christopher. *Warfare in the Latin East, 1192–1291*. Cambridge: Cambridge University Press, 1992.

Matarasso, Pauline, trans. *The Quest of the Holy Grail*. Middlesex, UK: Penguin Books, 1975.

Michelet, Jules. *Satanism and Witchcraft*. Trans. A. R. Allinson. New York: Citadel Press, 1946.

Nasr, Seyyed Hossein, ed. *Ismaili Contributions to Islamic Culture*. Tehran: Imperial Iranian Academy of Philosophy, 1977.

Nicholson, Helen. *Knight Templar 1120–1312*. Oxford: Osprey Publishing, 2004.

———. *The Knights Templar: A New History*. Phoenix Mill: Sutton Publishing Ltd., 2001.

Nicolle, David. *The Crusades and the Crusader States*. Oxford: Osprey Publishing, 1988.

———. *Knights of Outremer 1187–1344 A.D.* Oxford: Osprey Publishing, 1996.

Partner, Peter. *The Murdered Magicians: The Templars and Their Myth*. Oxford: Oxford University Press, 1981.

Paynes, Robert. *The Dream and the Tomb*. Chelsea: Scarborough House, 1991.

Read, Piers Paul. *The Templars*. New York: St. Martin's Press, 1990.

Riley-Smith, Jonathan, ed. *The Atlas of the Crusades*. New York: Facts on File, 1990.

———. *The Oxford Illustrated History of the Crusades*. New York: Oxford University Press, 1995.

Robinson, John J. *Born in Blood*. New York: M. Evans & Co., 1989.

———. *Dungeon, Fire and Sword*. New York: M. Evans & Co., 1991.

Runciman, Steven. *A History of the Crusades*. 3 vols. 1951. Reprint, London: The Folio Society, 1994.

Simon, Edith. *The Piebald Standard*. London: White Lion Publishers Limited, 1976.

Stern, Samuel M. *Studies in Early Ismailism*. Jerusalem: The Magness Press, Hebrew University; Leiden: E. J. Brill, 1983.

Strayer, Joseph R. *The Albigensian Crusades*. Ann Arbor: University of Michigan Press, 1992.

Turnbull, Stephen. *Tannenberg 1410: Disaster for the Teutonic Knights*. Oxford: Osprey Publishing, 2003.

Upton-Ward, J. M. *The Rule of the Templars*. Suffolk: The Boydell Press, 1992.

Wasserman, James. *The Slaves Shall Serve: Meditations on Liberty*. New York: Sekmet Books, 2004.

———. *The Templars and the Assassins: The Militia of Heaven*. Rochester: Destiny Books, 2001.

Weston, Jessie L. *From Ritual to Romance*. Garden City: Doubleday Anchor Books, 1957.

Wise, Terence. *The Knights of Christ*. Oxford: Osprey Publishing, 1984.

Index

Abbasid caliph, 133–34
Abraham, 20, 28
Acre, 75, 87–88, 91, 94, 120, 122, 127, 130–31, 136, 138, 147
Acts of the Apostles, 108
Al-Adid, 80
Al-Adil, 95
Al-Afdal, 86
Al-Aqsa Mosque, 37
Al-Ashraf, 138–39
Al-Kamil, 117–18, 120
Alamut, 69–70, 124
Albi, 101, 110
Albigensian Crusades, 101, 114, 147, 176
Aleppo, 63, 70–72, 134
Alexander the Great, 22
Alexandria, 28, 128
Alexius Comnenus, 30, 32
Alf ibn Wafa, 72
Alice of Antioch, 63
Allah, 19, 85
Almsgiving, 46, 162
Amalric I, 80–81, 83
Amanus Mountains, 64
Amaury, Arnaud, 114
Amaury de Lusignan, 143
Anagni, 147
André de Montbard, 43, 76, 78
Antioch, 20, 28, 34, 63–64, 69, 71–73, 75–76, 89, 135
Apace, 71
Apocalypse (See Revelation of St. John)
Apparellamentum, 108, 178
Arabs, 13, 19–20, 22, 113, 175
Aragon, 54, 56, 141, 161
Aral Sea, 124
Archangel Gabriel, 19
Archbishop of Bordeaux, 148
Archbishop of Caesarea, 75, 120
Archbishop of Nazareth, 75
Archbishop of Reims, 164
Archbishop of Rouen, 164
Archbishop of Sens, 164
Archbishop of Tyre, 121
Ark of the Covenant, 28
Armand de Peragors, 125
Armenia, 91, 133
Arsuf, 95, 135
Ascalon, 76, 78, 83, 88, 95
Assassination, 70, 72, 82
Assassins (*See also* Nizari Ismailis), 69–73, 78, 81–82, 95–96, 121, 124, 130–31, 133–34, 176, 179
  Syrian branch, 70–71, 81–82, 131, 135
Atlit, 115, 120, 130–31
Austria, 117
Avignon, 148
Aybeg, 130
Ayyub, 80
Ayyubids, 80, 96, 117, 121–22, 129, 134

Baalbek, 80
Babylonian Captivity, 148
Baghdad, 134
Baghras, 135
Bahram, 71
Baldwin I, 33–34, 36, 41, 56
Baldwin II, 36–37, 43–44, 60, 63, 66, 72
Baldwin III, 75–76
Baldwin IV, 83, 85

Baldwin, V, 85
Baniyas, 71
Banyas, 135
Baphomet, 157, 172
Baptism, 108
Barcelona, 122, 131
Baybars, 128, 135–37
Beaufort, 89, 135
Bedouins, 20
Beirut, 80, 88, 121
Bellator Rex, 147
Benedictine Rule, 46
Bertrand de Got (Clement V), 148
Bogomils, 105
Bohemond, 33–34, 63, 89
Bohemond IV, 121
Bohemond V, 121
Boniface of Montferrat, 98
Bulgaria, 101, 105
Burman, Edward, 45
Byzantine Church, 105
Byzantine Crusade, 76, 78, 100
Byzantine Emperor, 30, 32, 74, 85
Byzantine Empire, 28, 100

Caesarea, 135
Castile, 161
Castle Pilgrim, 115, 120, 141
Cat, 101, 162
Catalonia, 56
Catharism, 98, 108, 113
Cathars, 101, 105, 107–08, 111, 113, 147, 172, 176, 178–79
  The Perfect, 108, 111, 113, 178
Chastel Blanc, 135
Chivalry, 15–16, 19, 44, 49, 89
Christ, 22, 34, 36, 50, 108, 137, 159, 161–62
Christendom, 38, 95, 98, 100, 153, 166
Christianity, 12–13, 22, 28, 30, 33, 43, 49, 78, 82, 100, 119, 144–45, 164, 173–74, 176, 178
Church of the Holy Sepulcher, 22
Cistercian Order, 43
Communion, 15, 48
Confession, 15, 108, 162, 178
Conrad III, 75
Conrad of Montferrat, 91, 96, 98
Considerantes dudum, 166
Consolamentum, 108
Constance of Antioch, 64
Constantinople, 28, 30, 32–33, 75, 101
Cordova, 21
Council of Clermont, 33
Council of Lyons, 144
Council of Piacenza, 30, 32
Council of Troyes, 44, 56
Council of Vienne, 161, 165–66
Cross, 34, 67, 89, 108, 135, 155, 159, 162, 178
  Maltese Cross, 68
  Red Cross, 44, 51, 74
  True Cross, 88, 117–18
Crown of Thorns, 28, 36
Crucifixion, 34
Crusaders, 10, 34, 38, 53, 60, 66, 69, 71, 74, 81, 85, 96, 98, 100, 176
Cyprus, 94, 96, 100, 117, 127, 138, 141, 143, 161

Dai, 70
Dalmatia, 100
Damascus, 20, 60, 72, 75–76, 78, 80, 83, 85, 121–22, 124, 131, 134
Damietta, 117–18, 128, 130
Dark Ages, 101, 175
De laude novae militae, 49–50, 86
Devil, 46, 113, 157
Diego of Osma, 113
Dome of the Rock, 22, 37, 89
Dominican Order, 113, 151, 153
Dominic de Guzman, 113

Edessa, 34, 69, 73
Edward I, 136
Egypt, 20, 80, 93, 95, 98, 117, 129–30, 135
Endura, 108
England, 54, 56, 85, 91, 93, 95–96, 117, 133, 136, 141, 161
Esquin de Floyran, 151
Estates General, 161
Europe, 12, 14–15, 22, 43, 53, 73, 76, 85, 91, 94, 96, 101, 135, 141, 144, 146, 175
Everard des Barres, 74, 76
Excommunication, 30, 32, 48, 83, 98, 100, 119–20, 146–47, 161

Faciens misericordiam, 162
Fakhr ad-Din, 128
Fasting, 15, 46, 108
Fatimids, 73, 76, 80
Feudalism, 14–15, 18, 21, 38, 97, 113, 115, 144
France, 21, 33, 53, 56, 73–76, 85, 91, 93, 96, 101, 108, 110, 113, 117, 127, 133, 136, 141, 146, 148, 150–51, 153, 161–62, 165–66
Franks, 69, 71–73, 79, 83, 85, 88, 93, 95–96, 120–21, 124, 130, 136
Frederick Barbarossa, 91
Frederick II, 119–20, 122, 125, 128
Freemasonry, 10
Fulk, 60, 63–64, 73

Galilee, 117, 121
Gaza, 76, 93, 95, 125
Genghis Khan, 124, 133–34
Genoa, 22, 41, 122, 131
Geoffroi de Charney, 166–67
Geoffroi de Gonneville, 159
Gérard de Ridefort, 85–88, 91, 93
Germany, 74, 105, 110, 119, 130, 161
Gnostic, 172, 175, 179
Godfrey de Bouillon, 33, 36
Goliath, 173
Gondemar, 43
Grail, 16
Granada, 21
Great Schism, 30
Greek Orthodox Church, 28, 30, 108
Gregory VII, 147
Gregory VIII, 91
Gregory IX, 103, 113, 119, 121, 124

Guillaume de Beaujeu, 136–38, 141
Guillaume de Nogaret, 147–48, 151, 153, 161, 169, 172
Guillaume de Paris, 151
Guillaume de Sonnac, 127–29
Guy de Lusignan, 85, 87, 91, 96

Haifa, 115, 135
Hasan-i-Sabah, 69, 71
Hattin, 79, 87, 91, 117, 121, 125
Henry III, 133
Henry VI, 96
Henry of Champagne, 96
Henry, King of Cyprus, 141, 143
Herod, 28
Hohenstaufen Dynasty, 122
Holland, 117
Holy Ghost, 108
Holy Lance, 34
Holy Roman Emperor, 91, 119
Homosexuality, 103, 162, 172, 178
Hospitallers, 38, 72, 75, 79–80, 85–86, 88–89, 95, 117, 120–22, 124–25, 131, 135–36, 143–44, 148, 174
Huelgu, 131, 134–36
Hugh de Pairaud, 155, 161, 166
Hughes de Payens, 37, 43, 49, 55–56, 60, 66
Hungary, 117, 130
Hunting, 46, 80

Initiation, 157, 179
In Praise of the New Knighthood, 49
Inquisition, 48, 101, 113, 151, 154, 161–62, 179
Iran, 20, 133–34
Ireland, 161
Isaac, 28
Isabel I, 91, 96
Islam, 12, 19–22, 28, 73, 76, 80–81, 83, 85, 88, 96, 117–19, 128, 134–35, 145, 166, 176
Ismailis, 69, 71–72, 80, 82, 130–31, 133, 179
Israel, 10, 115
Italy, 33, 60, 85, 110, 117, 120, 161

Jacob's Ford, 84
Jacques de Molay, 141, 148, 151, 155, 161, 166, 169, 179
Jaffa, 41, 88, 96, 115, 135
Galilee — (see above)
Jerusalem, 19–20, 22, 28, 30, 34, 38, 43, 48, 56, 80–81, 89, 91, 95–96, 98, 117, 120–22, 124, 131, 136
Jesus Christ, 13, 28, 45, 108, 162, 173, 178
Jews, 10, 12–13, 28, 33, 146, 148
Jihad, 10, 80
John of Brienne, 119
John Comnenus, 73
John, Prince of England, 95
Judaism, 22, 172

Kaaba, 19–20
Karakoram, 134
Khwarazmian Turks, 124
King David, 173
Kingdom of Jerusalem, 60, 69, 76–77, 80, 87
King of Jerusalem, 36, 72, 85, 96, 119–20, 147

Kiss, Obscene, 101, 103, 155, 162, 178
Kiss of Peace, 108, 178
Knight Templar
  and Assassins, 73, 81–82, 121, 131, 176, 179
  and Finance, 52–56, 60, 121, 144, 166
  Chaplain Brothers, 45, 49, 66
  Chapters of, 47–49, 67, 74, 150, 157, 178
  Commander of the Temple, 139
  Expulsion 48–49
  Grand Master, 43, 66, 76–77, 81, 85, 91, 94, 115, 118, 125, 127, 130–31, 136, 141, 148, 155, 159, 162, 166, 170
  Head or Idol of, 157–58, 162
  Initiation, 48, 103, 172
  Marshal of the Temple, 86, 130–31, 138
  Master of France, 56, 60, 74
  Master of Ireland, 48
  Papal Privileges of, 82–83, 97, 141, 143
  Piebald Standard, 47, 49, 68
  Preceptor, 162
  Preceptor of Aquitaine, 166
  Preceptor of France, 127
  Preceptor of Normandy, 166
  Reception Ceremony, 47–48, 155, 159, 162
  Robe of, 44, 51, 74
  Rule of the Order, 43–45, 47–50, 56, 67, 75, 131, 150, 173, 179
  Seal of, 41
  Seneschal 76
  Visitor of France, 166
  Visitor of the Order, 152, 155, 162
Knighthood, 15, 18, 44–45
Knights of Malta, 38
Koran, 19, 80
Krak des Chevaliers, 72, 136
Kurds, 63, 80

La Forbie, 125, 127
Lambert, Malcolm, 101
Languedoc, 15, 101, 110, 113, 176
Lateran Council, 83
Latin Kingdom of Constantinople, 100
Lea, Charles Henry, 179
Le Chastellet, 84
Legman, G., 172
Lent, 46
Lévi, Éliphas, 157
London Temple, 54, 56
Louis VII, 73–76
Louis IX, 127–31, 133, 136, 144, 146
Lucifer, 101, 103, 107
Luciferian, 172
Lull, Raymond, 145, 147

Malikshah, 63
Mamelukes, 82, 128–30, 135, 137–39, 141, 143
Mangu Khan, 133, 135
Mani, 105
Manichaeans, 101, 105, 172
Mansourah, 128
Marj Ayun, 84
Martel, Charles, 21
Mass, 46, 48, 68, 108, 162
Masyaf, 72, 82, 131
Mecca, 19–20
Medina, 19
Medioramentum, 108

Mediterranean, 14, 22, 41, 52, 89, 120
Melissande, 60, 63
Mesopotamia, 20, 133
Middle Ages, 13, 172
Milites Dei, 68
Milites Templi, 67–68
Mongols, 12, 124, 129, 134–35, 137, 143
Mont Gisard, 83
Montségur, 113
Moors, 56, 74
Moses, 28, 114
Muhammad, 19–20, 28, 69–70, 117, 125

Nablus, 88
Naples, 141
Nationalism, 144
Nazareth, 120
Near East, 22, 179
New Testament, 108
Nile, 118, 128
Nizari Ismailis (See also Assassins), 69, 71–72, 81–82, 96, 135
Nosairi Mountains, 96
Notre Dame, 153
Nur al-Din, 76, 78, 80

Odo de Saint-Amand, 81, 84
Old Man of the Mountain, 70, 81, 96, 131
Old Testament, 107, 173
Omar, 20
Omayyads, 22, 73
Omne datum optimum, 66–68, 82
Ordo Templi Orientis (O.T.O.), 10
Oriflamme, 74
Original Sin, 12
Ottoman Turks, 135
Outremer, 60, 69, 73, 76, 79, 85, 91, 96, 120, 122, 131, 135, 137, 176
Oxus River, 124

Palestine, 22, 34, 38, 60, 76, 93, 117, 128, 136–37, 144
Papal Commission 154, 161, 164, 166
Paris, 44, 74, 148, 150, 159, 164, 166
Paris Temple, 148, 158
Pastoralis praeeminentiae, 161
Patriarch of Constantinople, 28
Patriarch of Jerusalem, 20, 37–38, 44, 75, 85, 120
Payen de Montdidier, 60
Peace of God Movement, 18
Pedro de Montaigu, 118
Pelagius, 117–18, 128
Penance, 49
People's Crusade, 34
Pepin the Short, 21
Perfect (See Cathar)
Persia, 20, 124, 135
Peter the Hermit, 33
Peter de Sevrey, 138
Phallic Worship, 172
Philip II, Augustus, 91, 93–94, 96
Philip IV, 136, 146–48, 151, 153, 155, 159, 161–62, 164, 166, 169, 172
Phillipe de Marigny, 164
Pierre de Bologna, 164
Pilgrimage, 10, 22, 28, 37–38, 52–53, 60, 64, 67, 80, 96, 121
Pisa, 22, 41, 122, 131

Poitiers, 148, 161
Polo, Marco, 70
Pope
  Struggle against secular monarchs, 15, 67, 97, 122, 146–48, 161
  Templars as private army of, 12, 67, 98, 120
Pope Alexander III, 83
Pope Benedict XI, 147
Pope Boniface VIII, 141, 146–47
Pope Celestine II, 67
Pope Clement IV, 136
Pope Clement V, 148, 161–62, 166, 169, 172
Pope Eugenius III, 68, 73–74, 78
Pope Gregory X, 146
Pope Honorius II, 44
Pope Honorius III, 115, 117, 119
Pope Innocent II, 66
Pope Innocent III, 97–98, 100–01, 113–14, 117, 119
Pope Urban II, 32–34
Portugal, 56, 161
Prayer, 15, 19, 45–46, 108
Priapus, 172
Provincial Councils, 162, 164, 166
Purgatory, 107

Qalawun al-Malik al-Mansur, 137–38

Rashid al-Din Sinan, 81–82, 96
Raymond II, 72
Raymond III, 85, 87
Raymond VI, Count of Toulouse, 113
Raymond, Count of Toulouse and St. Gilles, 33
Raymond of Poitiers and Antioch, 64, 72–73, 76
Reconquista, 21
Renaissance, 172
Renaud de Vichiers, 127, 130–31
Revelation of St. John, 22, 108, 117
Richard of Cornwall, 122
Richard I, the Lionhearted, 91, 93–96
Robert of Artois, 129
Robert de Craon, 66, 76
Robert de Sablé, 94
Robert of Flanders, 33
Robert of Normandy, 33
Roman Catholicism, 12, 22, 28, 43, 67–68, 103, 108, 114, 175
Roman Empire, 12, 20, 22, 28
Rome, 30, 66, 131, 146, 148
Ruad, 143

Safed, 121, 135
Safita, 136
Saint Sabas War, 131
Saladin, 80–85, 87–89, 91, 93–96, 115, 117, 129, 131
Satan, 13, 22, 103, 105, 107–08, 111, 172
Savelli, Cencio (Pope Honorius III), 119
Scotland, 56
Seine, 167
Seljuk Turks, 32, 63, 73
Serf, 14
Shirkuh, 80
Sicily, 119–20
Sidon, 88, 120–21, 139, 141
Simony, 49
Sin (See also Original Sin), 12, 49, 107
Sinan (See Rashid al-Din Sinan)

Sodomy, 49
Solomon, 28
Sophronius, 20
Spain, 21, 74, 113
St. Augustine, 101
St. Bernard of Clairvaux, 12, 41, 43–44, 49–50, 55–56, 66, 68, 73, 76, 78, 86, 113, 173, 179
St. Francis of Assisi, 117
St. John the Baptist, 108
St. Paul, 114
St. Peter, 46, 67, 159
St. Timothy, 114
St. Ursula, 158
Stephen of Blois, 33
Stephen, King of England, 56
Stephen, Patriarch of Jerusalem, 44
Stupor Mundi, 119
Sunni, 72, 80, 85
Syria, 20, 63, 70–71, 80, 82, 85, 121, 135, 143

Tancred, 33–34, 71
Tel Aviv, 41
Temple of Solomon, 37
Teutonic Knights, 120, 122, 131, 135, 174
Theobald of Champagne, 124
Theobald Gaudin, 139, 141
Theresa, Queen of Portugal, 56
Tiberias, 87
Tithing, 110, 146
Toron, 88
Tortosa, 141, 143
Torture, 12–13, 154–55, 159, 161, 164, 170, 179
Toulouse, 60
Tripoli, 69, 85–86, 89, 137
Troubadours, 15–16, 71
Turanshah, 129
Turks, 30, 33–34, 76
Tyre, 72, 89, 91

University of Paris, 155
Usury, 54

Vassal, 14, 148
Venerable Sanctuary, 22
Venetians, 98
Venice, 22, 41, 98, 100, 122, 131
Villeins, 14
Virgin Mary, 15, 43, 47
Vox in excelso, 166
Vox in Rama, 103

Walter de Mesnil, 81
William Le Bachelor, 48
William of Chartres, 115, 118
William of Chateauneuf, 131
William the Conqueror, 33
William of Rudrick, 134
William of Tyre, 80, 82
Witch Cults, 172
Worship of the Generative Powers, 172
Wright, Thomas, 172

Yves the Breton, 131

Zangi, 73, 76, 80
Zara, 100
Zoroastrians, 20, 175

ABOUT THE AUTHOR

Photo by Illia Tulloch

JAMES WASSERMAN is a lifelong student of religion and spiritual development. After attending Antioch College, he studied with various teachers of meditation and other disciplines. Settling in New York in 1973, he began working at Samuel Weiser's, then the world's largest esoteric bookstore. In 1977, he left to found Studio 31, specializing in book production and graphic design.

In 1976, he joined Ordo Templi Orientis (O.T.O.), having explored Aleister Crowley's system of Scientific Illuminism. In 1979, he founded TAHUTI Lodge, the third oldest O.T.O. Lodge in the world. He played a key role in numerous seminal publications of the Crowley corpus. In addition to his work on the Thoth Tarot cards and *The Holy Books of Thelema*, his book, *Aleister Crowley and the Practice of the Magical Diary*, first published in 1993, has been revised and expanded in a new edition.

He is also responsible for the widely acclaimed restoration of the Papyrus of Ani, *The Egyptian Book of the Dead: The Book of Going Forth by Day* published by Chronicle Books in 1994.

The Templars and the Assassins: The Militia of Heaven was published in 2001. Already translated into six languages, it is well on its way to becoming a modern classic.

The Slaves Shall Serve: Meditations on Liberty was published in 2004. This is his most controversial book. It provides an insightful analysis of the modern descent into collectivism and suggests steps to reclaim individual freedom.

The Mystery Traditions: Secret Symbols and Sacred Art, a revised and expanded edition of *Art & Symbols of the Occult*, was published in 2005. It is a celebration of the West's most beautiful esoteric art.

For more information, please visit:
www.jameswassermanbooks.com